HANDBOOK FOR COMMUNITY COLLEGE LIBRARIANS

	Information Behavior	23
	The Information Search Process (ISP)	24
	Modeling the Affective Domain	27
	Intervention Innovations: Learning Spaces and Embedded Librarians	30
	The Future of the Reference Desk	31
	My Story—A Reference Encounter	31
	Final Words	31
4	**Standards, Accreditation, and Supporting the Home Institution**	**33**
	ACRL Standards	33
	Your Regional Accreditation Agency	34
	Core Requirements	35
	Comprehensive Standards	35
	Other Licensure Activities	36
	American Association of Community Colleges	36
	My Story	37
	Final Words	37
5	**Information Literacy**	**39**
	History of the Information Literacy Concept	39
	Considerations in Instructional Programs	44
	Lens 1—Content Is King	45
	Lens 2—Competency Is Permanent	45
	Lens 3—Learning Readiness	46
	Lens 4—Personal Relevance	46
	Lens 5—Social Impact	46
	Lens 6—Relational Approach to Information and Learning	46
	Advocacy and Assessment	49
	Instructional Formats	50
	Knowledge Commons	50
	My Story—Contextual Information Literacy	50
	Final Words	51
6	**Instructional Design**	**53**
	Learner Characteristics	56
	Learning Styles	57
	Instructional Learning Objectives	58
	Teaching Strategies	59
	Distance Education	60
	Assessing Your Instruction	61
	My Story	61
	Final Words	62
7	**Managing Yourself**	**63**
	Paradoxes in Personal Productivity	65
	Time Robbers	65
	Project Management	68
	Managing Meetings	70

Making Your Emotions Work for You   70
Having the Conversation   72
Learning to Change   72
Developing Leadership   74
My Story   75
Final Words   75

8   Place, Budgeting, and Facilities   77

Library as Place   77
Exhibits and Displays   81
Facilities   83
Budgeting   84
Security   85
My Story   86
Final Words   86

9   Collection Development   87

Collecting   88
     Identifying   90
     Just-in-Time Purchasing and Publishing   90
     Selecting   91
     Acquiring   92
     Processing   94
Managing   94
     Organization   94
     Conservation and Preservation   94
     Collection Assessment   94
     Deselection or Storage   95
Unique Collections   96
     Archives   96
     Local History and Museums   97
My Story—Weeding Strengthens the Collection   99
Final Words   99

10   Diversity Considerations   101

The Scope of Diversity   101
     Ethnicity and Race   102
     Refugees and Immigrants   102
     Language Diversity   103
     Physical and Mental Health Challenges   103
     Learning Differences   105
     Gender and Sexual Orientation   105
     Generational Differences   106
Responding to the Challenge of Diversity   106
     Multicultural and Multilingual Librarianship 107
     Cultural Competence   107
     Using Emotional Intelligence   109
     International Community Colleges   110
Relationship Building   110

My Story—Being Open to What You Do Not Know	110
Final Words	111

11 Introduction to Technology — **113**

Document Production and Other Office Processes	113
Microsoft Office	114
Cloud Computing	114
Audio, Photographs, and Video	115
E-Learning	115
Tutorials and Games	116
Learning Management Systems	116
Webinar Presentation	116
Web Skills	117
Browsers	117
Search Engines	117
Websites	117
Library 2.0	118
Content Management Systems	118
Catalogs and Integrated Library Systems	119
Electronic Resource Management Systems	119
Discovery Systems and Federated Search	120
Digital Libraries	120
Institutional Repositories	121
Open-Source Systems	121
Personalized Information Organization and Management	121
Current Awareness Tools	121
Citation Managers	121
Note-Taking and More	122
Staffing for Technology	122
My Story—The Accidental Systems Librarian	122
Final Words	123

12 Assessment — **125**

Purposeful Assessment	126
Data Types and Methodologies	126
Using Your Results	128
LibQUAL+ and More	129
My Story	130
Final Words	130

13 If You Supervise — **133**

Skill Sets	134
Selected Concerns	136
Leadership	137
Strategic Planning	138
My Story	138
Final Words	139

Appendix A—IMLS Grant Proposal from 2010   141

Appendix B—The 21st-Century Community College Librarian
Survey Results   153

References   161

Index   171

ILLUSTRATIONS

LIST OF FIGURES

2.1	On-the-Job Skill Survey	15
2.2	Communication Competency	16
2.3	New Employee Skills	17
5.1	Wordle	48
10.1	Cultural Competence Model	108

LIST OF TABLES

3.1	Searcher Types and Their Personality Traits	28
3.2	The Information Search Process and Zones of Intervention	30
7.1	Time Robbers	66
9.1	The ACRL Collection Standards and Their Impact on Community Colleges	88
11.1	Microsoft Office Alternatives	115

LIST OF SIDEBARS

4.1	ACRL Principles	34
5.1	The Other Literacies	41
6.1	Standards for Proficiencies for Instruction Librarians and Coordinators	54
7.1	Sample Time Audit	64
7.2	Paradoxes in Personal Productivity	65

8.1   Community College Library Space Attributes and Needs   78
8.2   Atmospherics Checklist   80
8.3   Making a Catalogue   82
8.4   Book Jacket Quote   83
9.1   Collection Management Policy   89
9.2   Notes on Electronic Resources   93
10.1 We Are All Disabled   104
13.1 Suggested Resources   137

PREFACE

The genesis of this book was the authors' shared history working in community college libraries. We both currently work for the University of North Carolina at Greensboro (UNCG), a doctoral-level university of about 17,000 students; Michael Crumpton as assistant dean in the University Libraries and Nora Bird as an assistant professor in the Department of Library and Information Studies (LIS). The University Libraries and the LIS Department had jointly applied for and received a large grant, called the ACE Scholar program, from the Institute of Museum and Library Studies (IMLS) focused on bringing diversity to academic library staffs. In September 2009, we thought a similar grant could be proposed that would focus specifically on community colleges. One part of the grant was to look at the competencies necessary to be a successful community college librarian in the twenty-first century. A copy of the grant proposal from 2010 is included as Appendix A at the end of this book.

While in the process of writing the grant, we realized that the research on community college libraries was sparse. Community college librarians often do not have requirements to publish as part of their contract or tenure requirements. We felt that before we could educate new community college librarians, we needed to add to our own understanding of the environment and the skill set needed to succeed within it. We devised a wide-ranging survey that was sent to the Community and Junior College Section listserv. Partial information gained from this survey called the 21st Century Community College Librarian is provided as Appendix B at the end of the book.

We followed up that inquiry with focus groups with librarians from the North Carolina Community College Learning Resources Association. We launched the website Defining the Community College Librarian. We became particularly interested in the question of information literacy for vocational students and presented at conferences and wrote on that topic.

With our new understanding, we again wrote a grant application for IMLS funding with a shorter timeline. Although we were turned down again, we planned and offered LIS 652 Management Seminar: Community College Librarianship to UNCG LIS students. The outline for that course is the outline of this book. In 2013, shortly before the publication of this book, the authors were awarded an IMLS grant focused on diversity in community college librarianship. The curriculum, including LIS 652, will prepare ten students for the challenging role played by community colleges.

From the beginning, we shared a common view of community colleges as vital institutions that need competent librarians. We found in our survey that many of those already serving in that capacity had been doing so for more than 25 years, and many were ready for retirement. Part of the grant application had been the introduction of a special kind of internship, called Real Learning Connections, which would pair practicing librarians and student interns in a joint effort to learn. The proven model on which it is based is that the librarian teaches with specific learning objectives but so do the students by sharing their own expertise in technology, social media, and research with the practicing librarian. Each would acknowledge that they could learn from the other and create shared goals that could be accomplished together during the internship. Librarianship is at a generational crossroads, and the internship is the place where librarians and apprentices can meet and learn from each other.

We simulated these internships in an abbreviated way when we taught the community college library course. We incorporated a series of conversations between practicing librarians and students that the students had to report on for the class. It was wonderful to see those conversations deepen as we progressed through the semester.

This book is not simply a textbook; there is much more to it. The topics that we cover are certainly part of learning to be a community college librarian. We call it a handbook so that practicing librarians can feel that their work is represented here and that they could stretch their knowledge to incorporate new processes and procedures. We hope that every reader can learn new things about how to create collections, how to teach, and how to manage in the dynamic community college environment. We hope that we have succeeded.

General Description: With minimal supervision, this position will assist students, faculty, and staff by providing information literacy, introduction to resources, and library services. Functional responsibilities include:

1. Provide information literacy sessions in a wide range of subject areas for students in the classroom as needed or requested by faculty.
2. Provide instruction and training on the use of library resources, which could include print, multimedia, and electronic formats.
3. Provide public service functions in conjunction with other library staff including reference and research assistance, obtaining reserves and interlibrary loan materials, and general circulation activities.
4. Provide for cataloging activities as needed.
5. Update and maintain library's OPAC (online public access catalog).
6. Prepare and upload patron records and maintain exceptions.
7. Provide for physical processing of materials as needed.
8. Perform collection development functions for assigned areas.
9. Perform database maintenance and authority control in the bibliographic databases as needed.
10. Assist with development and maintenance of library website and related web based services.
11. Participate in policy review and enforcement of procedures related to library operations and resource procurement.
12. Provide service to the library through participation on various campus, regional, and national committees and/or task forces.
13. Participate in professional development opportunities in order to maintain current knowledge of the profession and techniques appropriate to library practice and procedures.
14. Supervise other library staff or students as assigned.
15. Oversee library operations and functions in the absence of the director.

Required knowledge, skills, and personal qualifications:

1. Knowledge of commonly used library practices and procedures as well as best practices for specific areas.
2. Knowledge of acquisitions processes and cataloging standards.
3. Understanding of basic concepts related to automated library systems.
4. Understanding of creation and use of web-based library services and instructional tools.
5. Ability to work in a diverse and dynamic environment.
6. Commitment to high customer service standards and teamwork with other staff.
7. Ability to adjust to a flexible work schedule as needed to maintain services, including evenings and weekends.

8. Ability to prioritize work to achieve the goals and objectives of the library and campus partners.
9. Ability to follow procedures consistently and achieve a level of detail.
10. Ability to use standard computer hardware and software.
11. Familiarity with interlibrary loan and reserves processes.

Required Experience: One year of work experience in a library, preferably at a community college. Teaching or delivering of instruction experience preferred.

Required Educational Background: A master's degree in library and information science from an American Library Association–accredited institution required.

- Technology knowledge, at least a basic level
- Technology access knowledge

Posting for Positions

Once identified by your organization, these competencies become the components worked into a position description and, in the case of hiring new librarians or staff, part of the posting for the position. It is important to invest the proper time and effort into this exercise because the hiring process starts with identifying exactly what is needed and creates the expectation of what an interested candidate can expect to be doing if successful. As mentioned earlier, community college librarians wear many hats and multitask extensively. The following sample job description contains many tasks and duties that might be needed:

This position description covers a very broad range of duties and skills that are desired and also establishes the complexity of such a position. Once it is agreed that this description is accurate, interview questions and processes should reflect the nature of the skills desired so that candidates can properly state their abilities. A posting such as this will also become the successful candidate's job description from which performance evaluations will be delivered.

Learning on the Job

One recent survey (2010) sought to find out what skills community college librarians gained through education and what skills they learned on the job. This distinction is important because as technologies and processes change, professional development opportunities are created but not always used. Learning sometimes occurs on the job as circumstances warrant, and this must be recognized so that those competencies can be incorporated into the administrative structure. As an example, one of the 2010 survey questions asked survey takers to indicate what skills were learned on the job versus in their academic training. Figure 2.1 is the chart with the results.

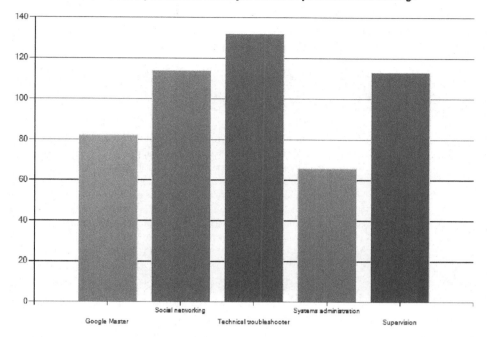

What skills have you learned on the job versus in your academic training?

Figure 2.1 On-the-Job Skill Survey

Many of the items listed were not part of library school curriculum, and still may not be, but represent important skills needed in order to effectively communicate and provide services to students and faculty. Anecdotally, it has been the authors' experiences that most emerging trends are learned on the job and not through formal means, which means those skills can be forgotten in the library's organizational structuring. It is also important to look at ways to invest proactively in professional development opportunities.

Professional Development

The previous position description demonstrates some basic and simple competencies needed by most community college libraries. In each case, individual librarians must determine their own competency needs for new hiring opportunities but also as ongoing professional development for current staff whose knowledge, skills, and abilities need to be updated or refreshed to meet the changing needs of the organization.

In 2009, WebJunction, an organization that supports learning opportunities for libraries with the support of OCLC and other organizations, published the Competency Index for the Library Field, which is available for free at http://www.webjunction.org/documents/webjunction/Competency_Index_for_the_Library_Field.html. This is an index, guide, and menu of competencies for the library professional. The purpose of compiling competencies for library practice is to assist librarians in all sizes and types of libraries in building the foundation of competencies to develop staff skills and knowledge and ultimately meet the needs of the

Communication

Clear and effective communication is the basis for success in your relations with co-workers, managers, users and all stakeholders. Communication competency is integral to customer services.

Competency: Communication	Communicates effectively using a variety of methods
Associated Skills and Knowledge	▪ Communicates openly and directly, both verbally and in writing ▪ Indentifies issues and ideas to be communicated and provides information that is accurate and timely ▪ Presents ideas in a manner that is clear and concise, with an appropriate level of enthusiasm ▪ Demonstrates proficient writing skills (good grammar and sentence construction, accurate spelling, logical thought) ▪ Demonstrates proficient public-speaking skills (articulation, strong delivery, appropriate animation)
Competency: Communication	Communicates effectively with a variety of audiences and individuals from diverse backgrounds
Associated Skills and Knowledge	▪ Speaks and writes in a manner that is professional, welcoming and appropriate for all audiences ▪ Demonstrates understanding of the perceptions, perspectives and communication styles of each audience ▪ Fosters an inclusive, affirming and respectful climate for communication
Competency: Communication	Selects and applies the most appropriate and effective communication means to meet situational needs
Associated Skills and Knowledge	▪ Communicates effectively to obtain consensus, persuade, instruct and/or motivate ▪ Understands and practices techniques of active listening and asking open-ended questions ▪ Selects appropriate communication strategies to manage conflict constructively ▪ Demonstrates negotiation skills to secure beneficial outcomes

Figure 2.2 Communication Competency

community. This can be a useful tool for developing a competency profile for your library staff. These competencies were compiled with input from a spectrum of library practitioners and leaders and cover the subheadings of library management (both personal and interpersonal), public services, technical services, and technology.

As an example, one of Giesecke and McNeil's (1999) core competencies of communication can be found in the Competency Index (see Figure 2.2).

It is not the authors' intention to list or recap professional development opportunities but rather to report on the importance of reflecting emerging trends and changing organizational needs in how staffs are developed and also how new competencies are incorporated into the organizational structure. This should be

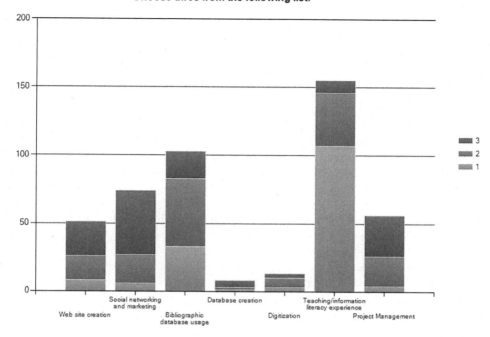

Figure 2.3 New Employee Skills

recognized through updated job descriptions and postings, which will also become part of performance reviews and the personal evaluation process. This provides the framework for an organization to keep up with trends and remain relevant.

Another question from the survey addressed the skills desired during a hiring process. As a benchmark for skills needed by the organization, when a vacancy is filled, new skills are typically sought out in the process and can become a new benchmark for skills needed by the entire staff. Figure 2.3 shows the types of skills desired based on new hiring—note these would not have been considered traditional skills in the recent past.

DEFINING A WORK CULTURE

The work culture of an organization can be a critical component to productivity and achievement of organizational goals and is developed from organizational history, traditions followed, values shared by staff, and the vision from which goals are developed. In a landmark article, organizational culture expert Edgar H. Schein defines culture as "(a) a pattern of basic assumptions, (b) invented, discovered, or developed by a given group, (c) as it learns to cope with its problems of external adaptation and internal integration, (d) that has worked well enough to be considered valid and, therefore (e) is to be taught to new members as the (f) correct way to perceive, think, and feel in relation to those problems" (Schein 1990, 111)

Libraries are an ideal workplace for culture growth and development, with many library mission statements rooted in traditional workplace cultural activities. Library mission statements, especially in academic and research-based institutions, will include references to library as place, as well as emphasizing the importance on the use of evaluating and using resources and gaining access to a broad spectrum of information both institution owned and freely available. Library staffs must not only be qualified in the use of resources and technology but also want to develop a culture that includes ongoing training, dedicated work ethics, diverse and tolerant points of view, and the ability to encourage creativity in each other and the patrons being served.

This means library staff should actively and consciously work to collaborate and pursue tasks together in order to enjoy mutual success. Schein also noted a work culture that is desirable to employees includes shared priorities, rewards, and institutional values that foster inclusion, high performance, and commitment, while still having room for diverse thought and action (Schein, 1992). The result is that each individual is responsible for contributing to the policies and procedures, and shared vision of how the organization functions and how it is perceived by patrons and other institutional staff.

This list of qualities and attributes that can measure individual commitment and buy-in could include the following:

- *Accountability*—provides a deep sense of personal responsibility in whatever task someone is asked to do or support

- *Effective Communication*—understand that communication is two-way, and work to make it smooth

- *Professionalism*—keeping personal issues out of the workplace is important to maintaining an objective and realistic point of view

- *Adaptability*—this is the ability to change and react appropriately to situations that occur unexpectedly or as a problem

- *Empowerment*—is a great skill to keep things moving

- *Quality*—high standards can ensure success for all

- *Collaboration*—approaching workloads as a team helps to ease the burden and keep everyone on the same footing

- *Recognition and Rewards*—recognizing and finding your own rewards for coworkers is a great incentive for their loyalty

- *Risk Taking*—provides excitement and motivation for moving the team forward

- *Commitment*—the workplace is where you spend most of your time outside of family, so being committed provides a sense of worth

- *Integrity*—high ethical standards are a must, and credibility can't be purchased

- *Continuous Quality Improvement*—learn to look for ways to improve all the time. Complacency and stagnation can be very tempting in this profession

- *Good Morale*—learn to feel and say to others what the positives can be

- *Service Orientation*—there is a great sense of service and satisfaction in providing service-oriented work

- *Courtesy and Respect*—is essential for good library staff to demonstrate that they are professionals

- *Stewardship*—important for maintaining and sustaining confidence

adaptation, similar actions can be employed in virtual modes such as instant messaging, chat, Facebook, Twitter, and e-mail. Research also shows that the emphasis must be on creating that connection with the user through explicit communication processes such as emoticons and responses that explain delays and process considerations (Kickham-Samy 2010; Radford 2006).

Use of these virtual services among college students is steady, but the decline in total library usage in this age group continues (De Rosa et al. 2011). So, it is imperative that librarians provide reference service in an ever-wider range of channels and promote library use through those avenues. Recent research indicates that while community college libraries do have a web presence, they do not include many interactive services such as blogs, user-created content, or RSS feeds that would contribute to relationship building (Pampaloni and Bird, forthcoming).

REFERENCE SUCCESS

Reference services were among the first library services to undergo regular assessment. Reference transactions were tallied every day, week, and year. For academic libraries, these statistics were once reported to the Library Statistics Program (National Center for Educational Statistics n.d.). Assessment will be discussed in more detail in chapter 7, but it is important to understand how transactions are counted and what makes them successful. In a reference transaction, according to the Reference and User Services Association (RUSA) of the American Library Association, the librarian must use, evaluate, recommend, or interpret information resources for a patron. RUSA does not include formal instruction or simple answers like schedules, locations, or policy interpretations (Reference and User Services Association 2008).

The number of transactions completed does not indicate the success of a service, however. A body of literature focuses on the often-quoted fact that the correct answer is provided by librarians only 55 percent of the time (Hernon and McClure 1987, 3), a figure arrived at by extensive, unobtrusive testing of librarians in many different settings. The librarians did not know that they were being questioned, the questioners already knew the answers, and only the information content of the answer was measured. However, the absolute correct answer to many questions is not always easy to determine; instead, the critical measure of a successful reference interview may actually be the quality of the user-librarian interaction. As Joan Durrance found in her studies on reference transactions, the strongest factors that influence a user's return to a library service are the librarian's expressed interest in the question, listening skills, and use of open-ended questions to clarify the user's question (1995, 258). In a setting that has a wide variety of students, making a connection with each student who requests help might be the most important work that a librarian does.

Information Behavior

The broad study of information behavior (Case 2002; Fisher and Erdelez 2005) covers information seeking, searching, and use and can be divided into three domains: affective, biological, and cognitive. The reference encounter could encompass all three modes of behavior. Affective issues involve the emotions of the information seeker, while cognitive characteristics manifest primarily in the understanding of the topic and the language used to describe it. Biological priorities, including physical issues (Kuhlthau 2004) and sensorimotor considerations (Nahl and Bilal 2007), involve the user interacting with the physical world of an information system and are often measured by the skill with which certain tasks, such as searching, are completed.

The bulk of this chapter's discussion will be devoted to affective issues, but it must be noted that in the community college the distance between users and the librarian can be based on cognitive issues, as well. Librarians have a master's degree and primarily speak English, which is also the language of many databases and popular Internet sites. When users do not know what the librarian knows, there can be a cognitive disconnect, and the reference interview negotiation becomes even more important.

The people who use reference services in libraries are looking for help to solve a problem. Information seekers are individuals. Though it may sound trite, no two people ask the exact same question. Even when an entire class is seeking the same resource to satisfy a particular assignment, the interaction between person, system, and resource varies. It can be easy when doing reference to stop at the provision of a resource and not pay special attention to each person. However, further exploration with the patron allows the librarian to ascertain whether or not that person has time to interact with the resource, if it can be read and understood, and if the person has the means to interact with it further.

A scenario can be used to illustrate the issues that might be encountered during a reference interaction in a community college. The user is looking for a discussion of Sigmund Freud's concept of the id. The librarian has created a wonderful guide to high-quality online resources that give good explanations of this concept and begins to show the patron these sites and then realizes that the recent graduate of the English as a Second Language program does not comprehend the text of the websites. Then the librarian realizes that the student is checking her watch every couple of minutes. The librarian asks about her time constraints and finds that she has to pick up her children from school. Then he tries to give the student a path to finding the online guide to take home with her, but she admits that she has no home access to the Internet. The student-information interaction will only be successful if the librarian can negotiate a return visit or print something quickly in order to give her something that she can take home to study.

Any one of these issues will be different for the next user coming through the door with the same topic question and the same purpose. However, despite the high level of individuality in each interview, research has identified attributes that can help a librarian provide high-quality reference service in the community college.

The Information Search Process (ISP)

One well-tested model of information behavior that works particularly well for community colleges is called the information search process (ISP). In her book *Seeking Meaning*, Kuhlthau (2004) examines a number of settings to uncover a series of stages that she describes as progressive. Some critics do point out that the work was primarily done with socioeconomically privileged participants and may not pertain to all students or workers, and that a better stance for community college

The future of library spaces has been discussed widely, and more will be said about it in chapter 8 (see, e.g., Stewart 2010; Millson-Martula and Spencer 2010). At present, some of the recommendations for changing spaces to diminish LA will be discussed.

Onwuegbuzie, Jiao, and Bostick (2004) list signage, layout, and a map handout as possible helpful tools. Technological innovations to mimic these suggestions could include the use of QR codes (Massis 2011) or maps that are downloadable to handheld devices. The authors do not discuss the possibility that similar dislocation can happen when the library-anxious user encounters virtual spaces such as the library's website. However, the principles of information architecture and work on virtual reference show that most virtual reference transactions involve questions about the use of the library's resources in cyberspace (Ryan, Daugherty, and Mauldin 2006).

- **Location anxiety or knowledge of the library**
  Each library is unique, and although many students may be familiar with their public library, they do not understand the college library or its information systems. Many do not understand self-service libraries, especially if they have recently emigrated from a different country where open stacks are uncommon and library resources scarce (Liu 1995). Many college students choose to go back to their public library rather than use the college library even though the resources there do not match what they need. Antell (2004) found that convenience, familiarity, and parking were contributing factors for this misdirected use, but so were the friendliness of the staff in the public library and a feeling of LA, especially for nontraditional students. Community college librarians should heed this lesson.

- **Mechanical anxiety or barriers**
  The skills needed to function in a library environment are in a constant state of change because technology is a moving target. In the past, librarians worried about teaching students how to use microfilm machines; now they want students to understand their catalog app for mobile devices. Each of these relates to the biological, physical, or sensorimotor skills that are required to use a particular technology or perform a multistep task. When students rate their computer skills, their self-assessment is higher than the scores they obtain on objective tests, especially with respect to information finding (Gross and Latham 2012). Although their skill with social media and even finding information is good, their ability to evaluate information is not at the same level (Head and Eisenberg 2010).

- **Resource anxiety**
  Jiao and Onwuegbuzie (1997) was the first to identify this dimension of LA, and it has particular relevance in the electronic environment. It is not that the item may be unavailable on the library shelf, but the e-book may be checked out to another user, or a student's password may have expired, or the item may not be owned by the library. This puts new pressure on students trying to complete their work in the allotted time. Many students turn to the most available and accessible item whether it matches their real need or not. Even worse, students may find a resource on something like Google Books and think that they have to pay for the resource when it is free at the library. Despite the availability of more free material, the complexities of resource accessibility are still a problem.

Table 3.2 The Information Search Process and Zones of Intervention (Adapted from Kuhlthau 2004 and Onwuegbuzie, Jiao, and Bostick 2004)

ISP Zone	Library Anxiety	Intervention
Initiation	Interpersonal	Information Literacy (IL) Instruction
Selection	Resource and location	Pathfinders
Exploration	Affective barriers	Virtual and Face-to-Face Reference, Embedded Librarianship
Formulation	n/a	n/a
Collection	Knowledge of the library	Instruction on reference managers (e.g., EasyBib, Zotero)
Presentation	Mechanical	Knowledge Commons

Intervention Innovations: Learning Spaces and Embedded Librarians

In *Seeking Meaning*, Carol Kuhlthau shows the areas of the ISP where interventions might lead to student success. Additionally, she posits levels of roles that the librarian might adopt, including that of information counselor (2004, 125). Unfortunately, information counseling has not found a wide acceptance in the library literature, but its meaning is clear for working in the community college environment. Table 3.2 attempts to summarize her recommendations and align them with the work on library anxiety covered in the last section.

Counseling and tutoring are done in specific spaces by qualified personnel, and they are rarely thought of as a library responsibility. However, community college libraries have long been regarded as the principal site for facilitating lifelong learning (Kalick 1992; Dowell 2006). Community college librarians were the first academic librarians to recognize that resources other than printed material might be helpful to learners, and in response many of the libraries underwent a name change in the 1980s and became learning resource centers (LRCs). As such, they housed film, video, and audio materials in various formats and collected educational software. The emphasis was on the materials and not on the services that went with them. The LRC name has stuck even though many of these materials are now digital and no longer housed within the physical confines of the library.

In response to innovations at many academic institutions, community college libraries are changing again. The learning emphasis has now shifted from simply providing access to materials to facilitating learning with expanded services. As noted in chapter 2, the administrative structures that include the community college library are quite varied: some library directors report to the dean of learning, academic affairs, or academic success. These structures often include academic support services such as writing and speaking centers, tutoring, and testing. Library space is being renovated into the information commons, learning commons, or knowledge commons. In many institutions, these spaces house counselors, tutors, or writing facilitators. These are the places where information counseling meets presentation counseling. Community college librarians should be prepared to be a comprehensive participant in student success.

Embedded librarianship is another innovation that can put a librarian in the zone where interventions are possible. Jennifer Ballance and other librarians at Central Piedmont Community College in Charlotte, North Carolina, came up with an

the Council for Higher Education Accreditation. This agency accredits more than 13,000 public and private educational institutions ranging from preschool to college level in the Southern United States. Your regional accreditation agency may be in another region, but its requirements will somewhat mirror SAC.

Higher-education accreditation is a type of quality assurance process under which services and operations of postsecondary educational institutions or programs are evaluated by an external body to determine if applicable standards are met. If standards are met, accredited status is granted by the agency. Here SACS will serve as the example of the standards established for institutional accreditation, knowing that other regions are similar.

In the case of SACS, the accreditation process will occur campus-wide every 10 years, and the library plays an important role. SACS Standards include core requirements and comprehensive standards, and the items pertaining particularly to the library are as follows:

Core Requirements

Core requirements are basic, broad-based, foundational requirements that an institution must meet to be accredited with the Commission on Colleges. They establish a threshold of development required of an institution seeking initial or continued accreditation by the commission and reflect the commission's basic expectations of candidate and member institutions. Compliance with the core requirements is not sufficient to warrant accreditation or reaffirmation of accreditation. Accredited institutions must also demonstrate compliance with the Comprehensive Standards and the Federal Requirements of the Principles, and with the policies of the commission, from the handbook for *The Principles of Accreditation: Foundations for Quality Enhancement* (Southern Association of Colleges and Schools, 2012).

The core requirement that affects the library is 2.9: "The institution, through ownership or formal arrangements or agreements, provides and supports student and faculty access and user privileges to adequate library collections and services and to other learning/information resources consistent with the degrees offered. Collections, resources, and services are sufficient to support all its educational, research, and public service programs (Learning resources and services)."

Comprehensive Standards

The comprehensive standards set forth requirements in the following four areas: (1) institutional mission, governance, and effectiveness; (2) programs; (3) resources; and (4) institutional responsibility for Commission policies. The comprehensive standards are more specific to the operations of the institution, represent good practice in higher education, and establish a level of accomplishment expected of all member institutions.

The comprehensive standard set forth for the library is 3.8, Library and Other Learning Resources, and is addressed with these components:

- 3.8.1 The institution provides facilities and learning/information resources that are appropriate to support its teaching, research, and service mission (Learning/information resources).

- 3.8.2 The institution ensures that users have access to regular and timely instruction in the use of the library and other learning/information resources (Instruction of library use).

- 3.8.3 The institution provides a sufficient number of qualified staff—with appropriate education or experiences in library and/or other learning/information resources—to accomplish the mission of the institution (Qualified staff).

OTHER LICENSURE ACTIVITIES

Schools will also obtain accreditation through national, professional, and specialized accrediting bodies, which is a voluntary system of nongovernment self-regulation standards. This process provides the forum for recognition by the U.S. Secretary of Education in which programs offered by institutions are evaluated for the quality of the education and training offered.

For this example, the community college system in North Carolina has a list at this link that includes both the applicable national agencies and the ones approved by North Carolina Licensing Authorities: http://www.nccommunitycolleges.edu/Proprietary_Schools/accreditation.htm

Your home institution can guide you further on local licensing and the requirements made of the library by each agency.

Heu and Nelson (2009), in their article on accreditations entitled "A Library Compliance Strategy for Regional Accreditation Standards: Using ACRL Higher Education Standards with Community and Junior Colleges in the Western Association of Schools and Colleges," discuss their perspective on conducting an assessment for an upcoming accreditation visit. They used inputs, outputs, and outcomes measures to highlight the difference in expected results between instructional programs and administrative and educational support (AES) units. In other words, they compared student outcome assessments with the AES unit's intention and ability to provide services and resources and cross-referenced them to the ACRL standards. This provided a comprehensive outline to methodically examine and analyze all library operations, services, and outcomes in the context of accreditation.

AMERICAN ASSOCIATION OF COMMUNITY COLLEGES

The American Association of Community Colleges (AACC) represents nearly 1,200 two-year, associate degree–granting institutions and more than 13 million students, as well as a growing number of international members. This professional organization (http://www.aacc.nche.edu/Pages/default.aspx) advocates for community colleges and focuses on five strategic action areas:

- Recognition and Advocacy for Community Colleges
- Student Access, Learning and Success
- Community College Leadership Development
- Economic and Workforce Development
- Global and Intercultural Education

As part of these strategic action areas, position statements are written to highlight and support specific components of the college. The last position statement regarding the libraries is from 2005, *Position Statement on Student Services and Library and Learning Resource Center Program Support for Distributed Learning*, and addresses some critical issues regarding library services that include:

- Ensuring inclusion for the diverse college population of differently abled students and faculty and the wide variety of levels and types of learners
- Meeting the 24/7 nature of today's study and work environments
- Accommodating disparate technology competency levels of on-campus and remote learners
- Adequately funding the technology infrastructure for the institution and the distance learner/remote user, as well as the distance learning faculty and staff
- Training faculty and staff and the distance learner/remote user in the "how" of successfully accessing, using, and, if needed, receiving assistance with online student support services
- Meeting state and regional accrediting guidelines for serving distance and remote users, as well as providing a variety of remote user support services and materials
- The full position statement is at: http://www.aacc.nche.edu/About/Positions/Pages/ps02102005.aspx. Another position statement from the AACC supports the information literacy goals of the Association of College and Research Libraries regarding information literacy. That statement entitled *AACC Position Statement on Information Literacy* encourages faculty to partner with the library or learning resources services areas to enable community college students to be information-literate lifelong learners (AACC 2008).

These elements certainly overlap with library values and standards. The full statement is at: http://www.aacc.nche.edu/About/Positions/Pages/ps05052008.aspx.

MY STORY

Accreditation visits can be scary; my first SACS visit was when I was only one year into the job. But the process of preparing for both an on-site visit as well as a document review was highly educational and useful in terms of learning about my new environment, as well as learning how the organization works and is successful.

FINAL WORDS

Accreditation and standards are critical to a community college's success, and the library plays an important role in supporting that effort. Any member of the library staff should have some familiarity with accreditation processes, and each will need to operate at a certain standard for the benefit of the college. In addition, each state or local area will have support on a larger level by library type to demonstrate consistency across the county. This link is for the Community and Junior College section of ALA, http://www.ala.org/acrl/aboutacrl/directoryofleadership/sections/cjcls/cjclswebsite, and provides information specific to the services and operations for community college libraries.

Locally, you should find other organizations whose purpose is to provide group support for the work of the community college library and library staff. In the example of North Carolina, we have a statewide association with a community college section, http://www.nclaonline.org/community-junior-college and a community college–specific group, that shares experiences and information about community colleges: http://nccclra.org/main/. In addition, many states have community college systems offices that can support individual college efforts.

competencies (knowledge, skills, and attitudes). The importance of media, Internet, and other information providers and their impact on the public's opinions, learning, and culture were debated at that forum (Media and Information Literacy n.d.).

NETWORK LITERACY

Social networks are the important parameter here. Network-literate individuals possess knowledge and skills using Facebook, LinkedIn, Twitter, and other social media.

TECHNICAL LITERACY—SEE COMPUTER LITERACY, DIGITAL LITERACY

TRANSITION LITERACY

Centered on the transition between high school and college, work in this area has touted the importance of cooperation between local high schools and colleges (Beaudry n.d.).

TRANSLITERACY

Rooted in a cross-disciplinary attempt to understand the new world of reading information in digital forms (Transliteracies Project n.d.), this concept has taken hold in the library world (Ipri 2012; Jaeger 2011; Thomas et al. 2007) because it reaches outside the library walls and incorporates all of the other literacy concepts described here. It remains to be seen how libraries will implement strategies that incorporate these multiple literacies, but beginning with information literacy is still a valid strategy.

In 2000, the Association for College and Research Libraries (ACRL) issued standards for Information literacy that entailed a substantial revision of an older document called the 1987 Model Statement of Objectives for Academic Bibliographic Instruction (Information Literacy n.d.). The *Information Literacy Competency Standards for Higher Education* are meant to encompass all levels of postsecondary education. Recently, more targeted standards have been written for science and technology, journalism, psychology, and other disciplines.

The difficulty for community college librarians is determining which of the standards applies at the two-year level for students who want to continue their education in the near future and which are important for those in the many programs offered. ACRL includes a *Community and Junior College Section*, but to date there has been no effort to tailor the competency standards for their particular needs.

The standards were written by librarians with libraries as the location for the resources to be used in exercises and assignments. The implementation of these standards in institutions is still voluntary, but the goal of information literacy has been recognized by organizations that do have a wider influence and more power to affect institutional change. Regional accrediting agencies, such as the Southern Association of Colleges and Schools (SACS) and the New England Association of Schools and Colleges (NEASC), have incorporated information literacy goals into their standards for college libraries. Many colleges have adopted information literacy as college-wide programs for their Quality Enhancement Plans (QEP), which are required by some of these agencies. Most importantly, in 2004, the National Center for Education Statistics added questions on information literacy efforts to their Academic Library Survey, which is conducted biennially. The questions now ask whether information literacy is an institution-wide objective, as these yes/no questions from the 2010 survey show:

Does your postsecondary institution have the following, or has it done the following:

800. A definition of information literacy or of an information-literate student?
801. Incorporated information literacy in the institution's mission?
802. Incorporated information literacy in the institution's strategic plan (If no then skip 803 and 804)?
803. An institution-wide committee to implement the strategic plans for information literacy?
804. The strategic plan formally recognizes the library's role in information literacy instruction?

The questions are an indication that information literacy is important beyond libraries, but the answers provided by community college libraries are not. In a small unpublished survey that the authors conducted, responses from 50 community college libraries indicated that only 50 percent had an institution-wide definition of an information-literate student, and only between 10 percent and 20 percent had information literacy initiatives built into the institution's mission or strategic plan. This shows that information literacy is still library-centric and has not become a priority for educational institutions in general.

CONSIDERATIONS IN INSTRUCTIONAL PROGRAMS

The standards provide descriptions that are an important but insufficient step toward the goal of producing an information-literate student. A validated set of criteria is elusive because it has become increasingly apparent that information literacy depends on context. How an individual assigns credibility to information resources is a learned social norm; a resource that is credible for one social group can be suspect for another (Nahl and Bilal 2007, 7). In the same way, individuals who possess information literacy in the fifth grade do not necessarily maintain it when they start to work within a certain profession in their twenties. Additionally, the skills required are a moving target. An information-literate person may be able to handle a particular Internet process at one time, but when the interface or the manner of accessing it changes, the ability to function may diminish or even disappear. For instance, someone who has been accustomed to the layout of the search engine Yahoo may be thrown out of her comfort zone when using Google, even though the two services are designed to accomplish similar information tasks.

Library and information science theorists have argued that the move toward information literacy has been self-serving for the library profession (Budd 2009) by artificially creating linkages to the teaching role in educational institutions (O'Connor 2009). Despite this criticism, information literacy activities are an increasing part of the professional work done in libraries (Lynch and Smith 2001; Walter 2008). The role must be reframed, however, to focus on how information is used to learn and work in the twenty-first century.

Reframing the purpose of information literacy requires a critical literacy orientation as pioneered by Paulo Freire (2000, 1994) that questions the use of standards that are meant to apply to every context (Swanson 2004 a, b). Troy Swanson bases his approach to the standards on research conducted in a community college, and he gives concrete advice for implementing a program that works to facilitate learning across the curriculum. He urges librarians to focus on the content and credibility of the information itself rather than the physical resources that are created from it, that is, books or encyclopedias. His ideas are echoed by David Patterson, who encourages librarians to think of equity when designing information literacy instruction in community colleges (2009).

When we begin to focus on the role of information in learning for all students in all contexts, then we have to use the standards in their most flexible way. Christine Bruce (2008) outlines a series of frames or lenses through which we can view the goal of information literacy. As we change the lens, the picture of information, content, instruction learning, curriculum, assessment, and information literacy itself changes. Each view has value, but when we limit ourselves to a particular one, we can be less than relevant to some students and their curricular contexts. One lens may work for an English as a Second Language student whose main concern is learning the American library system but will not work with a student who graduated from an American high school and intends to transfer to a university to complete his college degree. In the next section, Bruce's work is paraphrased to fit the community college environment (2008). The numbers do not reflect a hierarchy but make it easier to distinguish and refer back to each lens.

Lens 1—Content Is King

When looking through this lens, the librarian sees information as a commodity that can be transmitted. The content of instruction is the primary consideration, and all of it must be covered in detail. The librarian sees herself as an expert who can teach a package of instructions to students on how to find the resources that are needed. The students gain in the amount of knowledge they possess about the library, and once it is achieved it remains the same no matter how the context changes. The librarian can assess the gain in knowledge and can determine that information literacy has been achieved.

Lens 2—Competency Is Permanent

Information can be searched for and found if the level of skill is high enough. Content and context are less important than competence in the skills required. The librarian instructs students on how to find information, and students can perform this task regardless of what exact resources are needed and how they are searched. Instruction design is based on a determination of what skills are needed.

That level of skill can be measured, and information-literate students can be identified because they are competent in those particular skills.

Lens 3—Learning Readiness

Information is subjective for each student, and so the identifying characteristics of the informed learner vary accordingly. Using this lens requires that the instructor and the learner be collaborators in determining the content and the curriculum that are needed to achieve the student's goals. Because instruction is contextual and individual, assessing information literacy is challenging, but it can be assumed that an information-literate student will be ready to learn.

Lens 4—Personal Relevance

When information is valuable to the learner, it can be transformational. Content can be presented through scenarios and case studies that the learner can apply to other, more personal situations. The instructor is motivational and explains that information literacy skills will be useful in a variety of contexts. Assessing this type of instruction works best when viewing finished presentations of work that integrate the found information. Defining information literacy depends on context and the individual's own growth.

Lens 5—Social Impact

Information is based in a particular social or disciplinary norm. Content is focused outward toward how information can be used to improve social issues or problems. The librarian should challenge students to critically examine their own information restrictions and encourage them to look toward societal improvement. The curriculum and assessment are designed with a service-learning perspective. Information literacy is about shaping informed societal members.

Lens 6—Relational Approach to Information and Learning

The relational lens affords the widest view of information as objective, subjective, or transformational. The content of instruction would include critiquing a wide variety of sources and examining the student's own values in relation to that information. Librarians reveal their own views of information so that students can learn how to evaluate and make decisions about relevant information. The curriculum allows the student to become self-aware of methods for critical assessment. The transformation of the student's thinking is the focus of assessment. Information-literate students who master information literacy with this lens in place can apply information skills to a broad and complex range of situations.

Viewing the various user groups in a community college through these lenses can be beneficial to designing an information literacy program that is focused on every student's learning and academic success. One of the challenges for community colleges is showing that students can finish the programs that they set out to complete (American Association of Community Colleges 2012). If the library can be a factor in that equation, then it ensures its continued relevance and funding.

A full information literacy program, then, is looked at through these lenses at each of the constituencies that make up a college community. Using the ACRL *Guidelines for Instruction Programs* is a start, but other literature can help. Ragains (2006) writes a good how-to book with a strong chapter by Ann Roselle specifically on community college information literacy programs:

- **College-bound/transfer students**
  The library literature primarily focuses on this group. The ACRL guidelines recommend *Designs for Active Learning: A Sourcebook of Classroom Strategies for Information Education*. It is recommended that librarians work with English, writing, and other instructors to create strong ties between assignments and information literacy goals and vary them across different levels of classes.

- **Developmental students**
  Ann Roselle (2009) has written an overview of practices with developmental students that give ideas for how to work with the one-quarter of the college population that is underprepared for college-level work.

- **Early or Middle College Students**
  These hybrid programs vary widely from state to state. It is unclear in many of them what entity is responsible for information literacy education for these students. Collaboration with local high school librarians is a best practice in this situation. Moving these students to higher-level critical thinking will give them a real college education and prepare them both for work and for their next educational steps

- **English as a Second Language or English Language Learners**
  Articles on working with international students can help you understand how to build instruction for this divergent group (Amsberry 2008). Some will have advanced degrees that were completed in their home countries. Determining the best level at which to approach their skills in order to advance them is an important consideration.

- **Trades or Vocational Students**
  The difficulty here is that the context may be too difficult for the average librarian to fully understand. As noted by Bird et al. (2012), most librarians do not have a background in a trade or engineering specialty like heating, ventilation, and air conditioning (HVAC) or nursing. Yet these specialties do require special resources and information literacy instruction. One shortcut to understanding what information skills are required by a particular job is to look at O*NET, a jobs database provided by the Department of Labor. Each entry in the database lists the skills and abilities needed to do the job and the activities that are done by a worker in that field. Louise Klusek and Jerry Bornstein (2006) mapped these skills and activities to the ACRL standards for financial occupations. Preliminary work has been done on some vocational occupations using the same mapping strategy (Bird and Williams n.d.). In addition, using a word-mapping program such as Wordle on the words used to describe the occupations can be very revealing. Figure 5.1 shows a Wordle for the job-related activities for an automotive mechanic. The most prominent word is "information" because it was used the most often in descriptions of the job activities.

Figure 5.1   Wordle (created from O*NET descriptions of automotive mechanics activities).

- **Workforce Development Students**

  It is difficult to do formal training with these students because they are often involved in short-term duration classes. Yet they may be the group that most needs updated information skills and an introduction to specialized resources for the subject area that they are studying. Creating tutorials or short drop-in workshops that are focused on skills rather than resources can be a way to serve this population.

The best way to create contextualized information literacy is to collaborate with faculty experts in those topic areas (Grassian and Kaplowitz 2009, 276). Designing assignments that answer the faculty's learning outcomes while addressing information literacy goals is not only possible but has many advantages. As the relational approach lens indicates, the most flexible information skills can be transformational and can last a lifetime (Bruce 2008). If you show faculty that resource-based learning matches their own goals of building content knowledge, then both the librarian and the faculty member can win. Most librarians have good relationships with English faculty for many reasons but have a more difficult time with other disciplines. Some possible barriers that prevent collaboration:

- Fifty percent of instructors in community colleges are part-time. Part-time instructors have little time to explore the library, come to meetings, or meet the librarian.

- Most instructors have a master's degree, except in the vocational program faculty, where the rate is only 24 percent. Instructors without an advanced degree may not understand the value of information literacy. You have to use the language that they use to explain why developing information skills can be important.

- Working with program chairs is one way to get more general buy-in even from part-time instructors. If the program chair insists that information literacy be emphasized in every syllabus, then it becomes a condition that the instructor must meet.

- Individual faculty members may have poor or outdated information skills. Addressing training to faculty can help raise the value of your program.

ADVOCACY AND ASSESSMENT

How do you help your institution embrace information literacy? You must show that information literacy will help students succeed in their classes, their program, and, ultimately, their lives. UNESCO and the International Federation of Library Associations (Horton 2008) places information literacy in a continuum with literacy itself. Certainly, many people can survive without literacy, and they can certainly survive without information literacy, but then the question is, can they thrive?

One of the most compelling reasons that Horton (2008) provides for the international audience targeted by the UNESCO report is that new educational theories emphasize learning how to learn and think critically rather than memorizing. Learning to think critically is the essence of finding and choosing information sources that are authoritative and focused on a particular topic. The kind of instruction that fosters these skills falls under many headings including guided inquiry (Kuhlthau, Caspari, and Maniotes 2007, 2012), problem-based learning (Snavely 2004), or generally in library literature as resource-based learning (Grassian and Kaplowitz 2009). Assessing this type of learning is primarily done through the evaluation of the presentation portion of a project, an article, or an extended paper.

Information literacy is desirable, but it has not been tied to student success with validated measures except indirectly in the alleviation of library anxiety (Onwuegbuzie, Jiao, and Bostick 2004, 70). Devising ways to assess information literacy so that librarians can better determine the efficacy of their instruction has been difficult. Most information literacy programs use short before-and-after tests to look for the ability to perform information literacy skills (e.g., to find and cite resources). These quantitative measures can be useful to determine whether participation in a class has helped the student attain very narrow goals. But, as we have seen, information literacy is contextual. Whether the student has reached a general level of competence that can be called information literacy is another matter.

The Educational Testing Service (ETS) has created a comprehensive test called iSkills that can be used to measure some aspects of general information literacy (ETS n.d.). However, librarians rarely have influence over the implementation of such a test for all students, especially since there is a cost involved. The value of knowing how information literate any given campus is depends on the accrediting agency and how much or how little information literacy is incorporated into the mission. Unfortunately, it is not necessarily the norm for institutions to have made information literacy a priority. More homegrown methods of assessment are circulated on listservs, at conferences, and in publications. Remember that you should be assessing three areas:

1. Effect on student learning
2. Quality of the instruction
3. Appropriateness of the content covered

INSTRUCTIONAL FORMATS

As noted above, instruction can be synchronous (real-time), asynchronous (not at a fixed time but with deadlines), or hybrid. For synchronous instruction, in terms of numbers of interactions, most information literacy instruction happens one-on-one during a reference transaction either face-to-face or virtually. Group instruction has primarily taken the form of so-called one-shots (Grassian and Kaplowitz 2009, 130) that are offered as a short introduction embedded in a content curriculum course. These one-shots are sometimes library tours within a Freshman or First Year Experience course, and in other cases these classes focus entirely on information skills. Although many four-year institutions have adopted such courses, community colleges have been slow to offer them. The tide may be changing, however, since the push for students to complete their studies is so strong (American Association of Community Colleges 2012), and these courses are a proven mechanism for giving students a solid introduction to being a student and achieving success.

Asynchronous information literacy instruction programs are used increasingly to reach a larger number of students. Tutorials created with screen capture programs such as Camtasia or Jing are popular and easy to create. Potential for deeper learning experiences exists in computer-based, gamelike modules with built-in quizzes and other assessments. These are most useful when required for class credit and when accompanied by a pretest and posttest. Combining tutorials with interactive support such as an embedded librarian or an "ask-a librarian" program can put the library staff at the center of this activity.

KNOWLEDGE COMMONS

The knowledge, digital media, or learning commons is not simply a space but a concept that places information literacy in the center of the complex network of skills and abilities that are necessary to be a lifelong learner. By making the case that library-based resources are necessary for success, librarians can ensure their inclusion in the learning process. Familiarity with the many related literacies described in the other literacies box can help steer the conversation about the knowledge commons toward a learning resources–centered model of these important service spaces.

MY STORY—CONTEXTUAL INFORMATION LITERACY

I know all too well the problem of rubber-stamping instruction sessions. Many times the same student would take both English 101 and English 102 and have to come to the library for both. We administered a pretest and posttest, but they were on paper and couldn't be scored immediately to see if the student had to sit through the new session. So the same students had to do the same worksheet and wonder why they were wasting their time. In some particularly bad classes, the already trained students were belligerent about it. I know now that I should have used the experts to help the uninitiated through the short exercise. Or had them do something that was more meaningful to them. But when you customize a class, you often lose the ability to do a quantitative assessment. I do have excuses for not being more in tune with the class. Sometimes it was impossible to prepare materials for a single session because I was the systems administrator, responsible for two campuses, and trying to be involved professionally. From this safe distance I know that I should have engaged more with creating quality information literacy instruction, but there did not seem to be the administrative support from outside the library. Without the support of the faculty it is easy to ignore this most valuable of our many jobs.

FINAL WORDS

Finding and using information is an important set of skills for all undergraduates to achieve. It is important for all academic librarians to understand how to present these skills to their users and to determine if those users have been affected by that instruction. Community college librarians have a broad community of users that have been detailed here, and instruction must be targeted to each of them. In chapter 6, information is provided on designing successful instruction sessions.

6

INSTRUCTIONAL DESIGN

No matter how they are organized, community college libraries still fulfill a mission of instruction at some level within the campus organization. In 2007, the American Library Association (ALA) created *Standards for Proficiencies for Instruction Librarians and Coordinators* (partial list in Sidebar 6.1), which reflect the important but diverse nature of providing library instruction (Association for College and Research Libraries 2008). Most commonly, the library will be providing instruction on the use of library resources and addressing the basic foundation of information literacy by teaching how to evaluate information resources and how to use those resources appropriately. Thus, attention and purposeful preparation should be given to designing instruction to meet appropriate learning objectives and to support the academic mission and goals.

Some areas of consideration in instructional design include items such as:

- Teaching skills and methods to employ them
- Number of sessions and content to deliver
- Websites or tools available to be used
- Intended audience
- Teaching a skill one-on-one versus in groups
- Types of learner characteristics
- The teaching environment

Much has been written about learning and the processes by which the human brain translates and stores information and turns it into useful actions. For the purposes of a community college library instruction class, some basic assumptions should be made. These would include:

- Learning is a dialogical process (something that requires dialogue) either conducted internally or with others to consider different points of view.

Sidebar 6.1 STANDARDS FOR PROFICIENCIES FOR INSTRUCTION LIBRARIANS AND COORDINATORS, © 2008 ALA

5. Information literacy integration skills

The effective instruction librarian:

5.1. Describes the role of information literacy in academia and the patrons, programs, and departments they serve.

5.2. Collaborates with classroom faculty to integrate appropriate information literacy competencies, concepts, and skills into library instruction sessions, assignments, and course content.

5.3. Communicates with classroom faculty and administrators to collaboratively plan and implement the incremental integration of information literacy competencies and concepts within a subject discipline curriculum.

The effective coordinator of instruction:

5.4. Investigates aligning information literacy standards with the institution's program review, departmental learning objectives, and/or accreditation standards.

5.5. Collaborates with institution-wide faculty development programs to support ongoing faculty training.

5.6. Encourages, guides, and supports instruction librarians to collaborate with classroom faculty and administrators in the development of increased focus on information literacy whether at the course, program, department, or campus-wide level.

6. Instructional design skills

The effective instruction librarian:

6.1. Collaborates with classroom faculty by defining expectations and desired learning outcomes in order to determine appropriate information literacy proficiencies and resources to be introduced in library instruction.

6.2. Sequences information in a lesson plan to guide the instruction session, course, workshop, or other instructional material.

6.3. Creates learner-centered course content and incorporates activities directly tied to learning outcomes.

6.4. Assists learners to assess their own information needs, to differentiate among sources of information, and to develop skills to effectively identify, locate, and evaluate sources.

6.5. Scales presentation content to the amount of time and space available.

6.6. Designs instruction to best meet the common learning characteristics of learners, including prior knowledge and experience, motivation to learn, cognitive abilities, and circumstances under which they will be learning.

6.7. Integrates appropriate technology into instruction to support experiential and collaborative learning as well as to improve student receptiveness, comprehension, and retention of information.

The effective coordinator of instruction:

6.8. Identifies, encourages, and supports training opportunities for librarians in instructional design and incorporating technology to support pedagogy.

Used by permission of the Association for College and Research Libraries.

- Learning is cyclical, as learning outcomes affect or influence the next learning experience.
- Learning occurs through individual lenses and experiences; thus, learning outcomes can be different for each person.
- Learners have preferred strategies for learning.
- Learning takes place within a context.
- Learning is affected by emotions.

These assumptions impact teaching methods and strategies as well as technology used or level of content presented.

The principles of setting a context for learning have been investigated in several papers by M. David Merrill, an instructional effectiveness consultant (see, e.g., Merrill 2002) Merrill identified these principles for facilitating learning:

- Learners are more engaged when solving real-world problems.
- Activating existing knowledge is the best foundation for new knowledge.
- Demonstrating their new knowledge by applying it immediately solidifies learning for students.
- Work that integrates old and new knowledge solidifies learning.

To achieve this he suggests four phases of design: activation, demonstration, application, and integration. Each of these phases would have tasks developed in components or modules that provide specific learning targets and corresponding learning objectives. In information literacy instruction, an example would involve these steps: how to provide information, explaining how to access information, discussion of how to make information comparisons or evaluate resources, and then, perhaps, the proper use of the information obtained.

Merrill also advocates a blended approach to introducing materials used for teaching and the activities by which learning occurs. This occurs by identifying each of these separately, but merging concepts that integrate both. His concepts and some examples in our discussion are:

Navigation
- Learners need to know how materials and contents are organized and accessed.
- Learners should be able to access and maneuver through resources and correct themselves as needed to understand mistakes.

Motivation
- Learning sessions and activities must be interesting and relevant.
- Examples used should be real and practiced.
- When basic elements are not motivating, students should be able to skip over them and move on to the place where they are challenged by the material.
- Performing entire research projects is more motivating then decontextualized actions or examples.
- Time for reflection and practice offers motivational delayed gratification.

Collaboration

- The use of small group interactions encourages a better-quality discussion.
- Group assignments should be structured around tangible outcomes as outlined by the main course instructor.

Interaction

- Interaction means solving real-world problems or tasks.
- Students should discuss methods used within activities provided.
- Key elements to interact with are context, challenges, learning activity, and feedback.

Merrill considers his first principles of instruction like a "pebble in the pond" where the point at which the pebble drops is the problem to be solved, which then creates radiating circles or ripples in the different methods used in designing instruction. For community college librarians who have limited time and exposure to teaching classrooms of students, investment in developing good basic instructional principles can be critical.

LEARNER CHARACTERISTICS

A starting point for deciding what design elements are needed is to determine who the learner or groups of learners are and what characteristics define them. General characteristics to consider would be gender, age, ethnicity, and experiences. An example might be a beginning English class in which, by definition of being in that class, learners can be presumed to have similar experiences or characteristics at that point in time related to the subject matter or level of instructional need. In the beginning community college English class, certain assumptions can be made regarding core academic levels of understanding coming from high school. In this case, knowing academic curriculum standards for your particular institution might give an indication as to the differences in students assigned to beginning English as opposed to those who start at a higher level based on their high school experience.

Students will also be coming to your library instruction classes with preconceived notions or ideas about information literacy and about the subject-oriented assignment that they have in hand. Once again, this is an opportunity to determine within the scope of your community what the expectations of students coming out of high school are or what exposure they have had up to this point with the materials you expect to cover. This includes identifying their current knowledge, skills, and abilities (KSAs) in order to determine more closely the instructional need.

Morrison, Ross, and Kemp identify several categories of learner characteristics to consider including previous academic experience and exposure to similar learning objectives. These are:

- Personal and social characteristics such as age and maturity, work or other real life experiences, motivational factors, and technical dexterity;
- Cultural diversity as a factor here in order to ensure a common understanding of information and materials being presented;

- Learners with disabilities must be given consideration based on their needs. Most community colleges have disability support programs that will aid in providing assistance for students who need them.

- Adult learners also have specific learning characteristics that need to be addressed in the design process, and it is important to recognize that this group of individuals could be very different than students who come directly from high school. Their background includes real-life experiences that may help them understand the material, but their exposure to the use of technology and the use of information for academic work could be limited.

All of these characteristics and any other distinguishing factors should be considered in preparing for an instructional class. Some elements of instruction including the exact parameters of the assignment might come from the primary instructor, as well. This is a great opportunity to partner with the primary course instructor on the design of the session or sessions.

LEARNING STYLES

Learning styles are an important consideration in library instructional classes because you can expect students to have a broad range of effective learning patterns. For example, some students are going to be visual learners, which means they will learn more effectively with visual representations of the content, or they might be kinetic learners, which means they learn better by working directly with a sample exercise. A learning style may affect learning more than you realize; new research on the brain shows that different stimuli will activate different parts of the brain. If you do not teach to a particular student preference during your limited time with them, then you may not deliver the important content that you want to impart. Considering different styles as you design the content of your presentations will help you activate students' whole brain so that they are fully engaged and learning.

There are many different inventories of learning styles, but the three basic ones are as follows (see "Learning Styles Online.com" 2012 for more information):

- *Visual*—An old aphorism says that a picture is worth a thousand words. For visual learners, that is especially apt. The brain processes visual information through the temporal and parietal lobes. These also manage spatial orientation. When you are trying to show students how to navigate the physical library, using visual material is essential.

- *Aural*—Hearing information is better for some students, especially those who come from cultures without a history of written information. The temporal lobes handle aural information in the brain.

- *Kinesthetic*—Activating students' cerebellum and motor cortex can help them be ready to apply what they learned in a new setting.

In addition to these three, other ways of learning are sometimes described. These are (see "Institute of Learning Styles Research" 2013):

- *Interactive (or social)*—Group activities are especially meaningful to students who prefer this style. When engaged in group activities, the limbic systems are

involved, which includes emotional centers of the brain. Group work can be difficult to manage because of these emotional associations.

- *Print (or logical)*—When students interact with print, they use the logic centers, or parietal lobes, of the brain. Most education is delivered through print, but many community college students were not successful in that mode. Designing instruction with these other elements might be more successful.
- *Haptic*—This mode is related to kinesthetic learning. Drawing and other work with the hands is important to these learners.
- *Olfactory*—The sense of smell is rarely considered in educational settings but can provide some of our most memorable experiences. How many times have you talked with someone about the smell of old books? Associating the smell of cookies with library instruction, for example, might work with these students.
- *Solitary*—A preference for learning alone is not popular in teaching circles anymore, but some students prefer work that they can accomplish on their own. Giving a short assignment that can be completed individually on the student's own time can help bridge that gap.

One of the more popular authors of learning style theory is David Kolb (1984), who discusses a four-stage learning cycle in which the learner "touches all the bases." He sees these cycles as:

- *Concrete Experience*—A new experience or situation is encountered, or a reinter-pretation of existing experience begins.
- *Reflective Observation*—Reflecting on the new experience. Of particular impor-tance are any inconsistencies between experience and understanding.
- *Abstract Conceptualization*—Reflection gives rise to a new idea, or a modification of an existing abstract concept.
- *Active Experimentation*—Learners apply the new ideas to the world around them to see what results.

For a library instruction class or series of classes, the purposeful use of these learn-ing style elements in the design of the class could significantly influence the learning outcomes.

INSTRUCTIONAL LEARNING OBJECTIVES

The next consideration for instructional design are the learning objectives for any particular class. This is also where partnership or collaboration with the course instructor will be critical. But some librarians provide general instruction sessions, and these too should have learning objectives developed and assigned. Here are some questions (Morrison, Ross, and Kemp 2004) to consider in getting started:

- What is the purpose of this instruction?
- How can learners demonstrate their understanding of the material?
- How can you assess whether learners mastered the content?
- What specific content and performance are expected as a result of the instruction?

Morrison, Ross, and Kemp (2004) also identify three important reasons for why the development of objectives is important for instructional design. First, the objectives clarify the resources and activities needed to make learning effective. This gives the instruction clear purpose and focus. Next, addressing the function of evaluation helps to develop a framework for learning and a means of measuring achievement. Finally, the function of guiding the learner gives the means to identify the skills and knowledge needed to master the information. Stated a little differently, the important functions of learning objectives to library instruction classes would be:

- Appropriate and applicable design of materials
- Evaluation and assessment of learning
- Providing structure for the student

This is the essence of how an instruction class should be structured around these functions.

Writing these objectives becomes another important task in order to ensure that instruction time is not wasted but used efficiently. The primary faculty member becomes your subject matter expert for blending subject expertise with library resources and guidelines. Objectives should also include behavioral objectives, or how students can demonstrate their learning, the use of action verbs, and the expected level of achievement.

TEACHING STRATEGIES

As library instruction has changed over the years from basic bibliographic instruction on print resources to more dynamic forms of instruction, a wide range of electronic resources and teaching strategies have evolved as well. Support for distance education courses has also added complexity to library instruction expectations along with the strategies and methods employed by instructional librarians. Strategies and methods are no longer one-size-fits-all; different disciplines and subjects have different expectations for the way in which library instruction is conducted. Resources like tutorials and consolidated resource portals such as LibGuides are now customized for different subject needs.

Teaching strategies and methods should not only be customized for different groups and types of needs, but also should use a variety of content delivery methods to engage students based on learning styles. This also means that in any given group of students you can expect to address several different styles with different methods of instruction. For example, a lecture (abstract) on evaluating resources could also include a demonstration (concrete) with some practice time built in (active) and finally a write-up of the experience (reflective). The use of visuals, media clips, and guest speakers also engages multiple senses.

In developing your teaching strategies or methods, the library literature is full of articles related to learning instruction, styles, and strategies. Even though library instruction is a big part of librarians' responsibilities, library school programs cannot fully prepare librarians for teaching. Some librarians are natural teachers; however, the majority of librarians at the beginning of their careers experience inadequacy and frustration in teaching. To fulfill the need for library instruction education, experienced librarians have written many books on the topic, and *Practical Pedagogy for Library Instructors: 17 Innovative Strategies to Improve Student Learning*, edited by Cook and Sittler (2008) offers a well-rounded point of view.

This volume focuses on two major philosophical orientations: direct instruction and student-centered learning. The editors believe that understanding these two styles will help library instructors understand how students learn, make better decisions about how to teach, and, as a result, achieve improved learning outcomes. A general overview of pedagogical theories is given, followed by a discussion of how they relate to student learning and a comparison table of "Direct Instruction" versus "Student-Centered Learning" in a variety of aspects: purpose, learning outcome, role of student, role of teacher, instructional strategies, and examples. The table is followed by an explanation of each one of the aspects.

The book includes seven case studies of librarians using the direct instruction approach to teach a large amount of information and complex ideas to groups of students; in each of these cases, direct instruction was the best approach to use to deliver the information. The cases present effective ways to teach the research process. For example, one of them uses metaphors as tools to increase student understanding. Another uses storytelling as an effective tool for increasing student understanding of complex concepts. The last nine chapters include examples of student-centered learning, where the librarian is less focused on delivering specific knowledge than on active learning in a group setting. This type of technique allows students to use their own experiences as a basis for new information literacy skills.

Another resource to consider is LOEX, a self-supporting, nonprofit educational clearinghouse for library instruction and information literacy information. It provides information on all aspects of instruction and information literacy to libraries and librarians who are institutional members of LOEX. For community colleges that are in close proximity to larger universities, consortium or collaborative-type agreements with regard to resource sharing or buying are common. This is also an opportunity to collaborate on instructional strategies, especially if there is a high chance that the institutions will share the same students over time.

DISTANCE EDUCATION

In designing instruction, it is now important to consider distance education coursework, which is an ongoing trend in higher education. In fact, course delivery via distance education methods is becoming more sophisticated and ensuring that the library is a component more important than ever. Librarians working with distance education instruction need to consider this type of instruction more different than the seated counterpart and recognize that different competencies are needed.

In their book *Advanced Methods in Distance Education*, Dooley, Lindner, and Dooley (2005) identify six core competencies that are needed for successful distance education learning: understanding adult learning theory, having the technical knowledge needed, knowing how the instruction is designed, relating to communication skills in a virtual environment, using graphic design to support learning, and administrative issues. The point is that conducting library instruction online or virtually will require modification or differentiating the design of the instruction. Technical skills, the use of visuals, how you communicate as an instructor are some of the considerations that should be made in order to ensure the instruction is effective.

ASSESSING YOUR INSTRUCTION

Donald Kirkpatrick's *Four Levels of Training* (1998) has been an industry standard in evaluating training programs for many years. Kirkpatrick's concept of four levels of evaluation applies to the type of instructional activities associated with library instruction. The four levels of the author's evaluation model essentially measure:

- *Reactions*—What they thought and felt about the training
- *Learning*—The resulting increase in knowledge or capability
- *Transfer*—Extent of behavior and capability improvement and implementation or application
- *Results*—The effects on the business or environment resulting from the trainee's performance

On his diagrammed pyramid, the reaction to training or learning represents the broadest area of data to work with and narrows accordingly so that the ultimate learning evaluation becomes the end result or the impact on performance. In the case of community college students, the impact that library instruction has on their academic performance overall is the crucial, but very difficult to measure, factor.

Many case studies exist that recognize the unusual nature of library instruction because in most cases there is no formal requirement that the student obtain these skills. Student learning outcomes for library instruction and information literacy are typically vetted through individual curriculum coursework and academic instructors in terms of motivating students with grades or academic standings. Some models are starting conduct "for credit" instruction through the library as well as having an information literacy outcomes assessment included in the larger scope of a student's academic experience.

Sheril Hook conducted a research project in which she reviewed three years of literature to determine if library instruction makes a difference in an academic environment. In her article published in *College & Research Libraries* (2012), she happily concluded that there is a positive relationship between library instruction and overall student learning outcomes. Qualitative evaluation and not just keeping track of numbers (sessions or students) provides a more meaningful approach to ensuring that the library is part of the academic experience and the institutional learning objectives.

MY STORY

During my first SACS visit, I recognized that the focus of our information-gathering efforts were on quantitative measures, specifically in instruction, with the number of instructional sessions presented and the number of students attending recorded. We were under the new SACS standards by then and immediately began assessing learning outcomes differently for our instruction classes, which resulted in changes to the design of our sessions as well. By redesigning and assessing outcomes differently, we gained more interaction and respect from the academic faculty, as well as a successful accreditation visit from SACS.

FINAL WORDS

As a conclusion and review, we look at the ADDIE model for instructional design, as it is a generic process used by libraries across the country to help grow and develop the instructional component of library services. This model was originally developed at Florida State University and can act as a guideline for designing and implementing instructional activities.

The ADDIE (Analysis, Design, Development, Implementation, and Evaluation) instructional design model is the traditional process used by instructional designers and training developers. There are five steps or phases:

- *Analysis.* In the analysis step, the instructional need or problem is identified and addressed by establishing instructional goals and objectives. This also includes a review or analysis of the learning environment and learner's existing knowledge and skill sets.

- *Design.* In the design step, learning objectives, assessment instruments, exercises, content, subject matter analysis, lesson planning, and media selection are developed and strategically planned. This design phase is systematic and specific. With regard to library instruction, in this step, content instructors should be consulted for their input on possible assignments and how learning objectives can be assessed.

- *Development.* In the development step, instructional designers and developers create and assign content materials selected earlier. In this step, if e-learning is involved, programmers work to develop and/or integrate technologies.

- *Implementation.* During the implementation step, procedures for training both the instructors and the learners are developed. The instructors' training should cover the course curriculum, learning outcomes, method of delivery, and testing procedures.

- *Evaluation.* The evaluation step consists of two parts: formative and summative. Formative evaluation should occur in each step of the ADDIE process. Summative evaluation consists of tests designed for specific criteria and referenced items and providing opportunities for feedback from the users.

ADDIE represents a dynamic, flexible guideline for building effective training and performance support tools and could be a great tool for designing your own instruction in your institution.

7

MANAGING YOURSELF

Chapter 2 discussed the wide range of tasks that community college librarians can be called upon to perform. Because of the eclectic nature of duties and responsibilities, time management becomes an important quality of a successful library staff member. Managing time can be viewed in multiple ways, both personally by individuals and also in how library staff members work together to take advantage of operational efficiencies. From time to time, special projects, events, or requests will cause staff to engage in project management principles. This chapter will cover personal productivity issues, team collaborative techniques, and project management principles that apply to community college library environments.

These are just a few of the quotes that can be found regarding time management myths and beliefs:

- "Planning my time just takes more time."
- "Time management problems mean that I don't have enough time to get done what needs to be done."
- "The busier I am, the better I'm using my time"

In reality, everyone has the same amount of time; it's how you spend it that makes a difference. Understanding how you spend your time is critical for making decisions on how to spend it wisely. Here are some options to help determine how to spend your time:

- *Tools:*
  - Time logs—Measure activities
  - Time audits—15-minute segments
  - Activity scheduler

Sidebar 7.1   SAMPLE TIME AUDIT

Time Audit

Task/activities	Time spent	Relevant?

This is a basic worksheet to track how you spend time. An honest appraisal of all activities, including time spent on nontasks, added together could be revealing as to where all of your time goes each day. And looking back at your Time Audit sheet, you could ask yourself the following questions:

• Can you see any patterns in your behavior?
• Are there times when you have left tasks before completion to do other things?
• Are you distracted easily?
• How many times were you interrupted during tasks?
• How could you have avoided interruptions?
• Were your actions relevant?

• *Calendars:*
  • Lotus Notes/Outlook—Knowing the features available
  • Google calendar—Does it work for you?
  • Overuse of calendars—How many is too many?
• *Your performance:*
  • Performance management plans or review tools—Where is the time spent?
  • The boss—How aware of your time is your supervisor?

Multiple time management tools can be found on the web; the key is to find a tool that fits your situation and allows an honest appraisal of how you spend your time in small increments over the course of a day or days. If you complete an audit or a log honestly, you might find that certain things or activities are taking up more time that you realize. This includes socializing and other activities that are not directly related to work time but have an impact on your day, which can help you determine if your time is being spent productively. See Sidebar 7.1 for examples.

Calendars are also tools to help you manage your time by coordinating schedules and events in order to provide planning opportunities. It is not uncommon for individuals to keep multiple calendars and be part of others' calendars in a working group, but overuse of calendars can also affect your productivity. Use the right number of calendars to be efficient, such as one for work and one for social activities, but not so many that you are spending more time managing the calendar than managing the activities the calendar is there for. Also be aware of your calendar's features so as to take advantage of tools and options that will maximize your use of the tool.

Sidebar 7.2 PARADOXES IN PERSONAL PRODUCTIVITY

Open–Door Paradox—By leaving a door open in hopes of improving communication, staff can increase the wrong kind of communication, meaning of a trivial or socializing nature. This multiplies interruptions and distracts from more important tasks. The "open door" was intended to mean "accessible," not physically open.

Planning Paradox—People often fail to plan because it takes time to prepare; then they fail to recognize that effective planning saves time in the end.

Tyranny–of–the–Urgent Paradox—Folks who just want to put out fires tend to respond to the urgent rather than the important matters. Thus, long-range priorities are neglected, which reduces productivity and growth.

Crises Paradox—Some people tend to overrespond to crises, thereby making them worse.

Meeting Paradox—By waiting for latecomers before beginning a meeting, we penalize those who came on time and reward those who came late.

Long–Hour Paradox—The longer hours people work, the more fatigued they become, and the longer they assume they have to complete tasks. But quantity doesn't always beat quality.

Activity vs. Effectiveness Paradox—People tend to confuse efficiency with effectiveness. They will be more concerned about doing the job right than about doing the right job. No matter how efficiently a job is done, if it is the wrong job, it will not be effective.

Do–It–Right Paradox—You never have time to do it right the first time, but you always have time to do it over.

PARADOXES IN PERSONAL PRODUCTIVITY

A *paradox* is a statement that is contradictory to how events really are, *personal* is about how you spend your time, and *productivity* is about producing goods or services. *Personal productivity* is defined as your time spent to produce goods and services (performing your work), so paradoxes in personal productivity are activities that appear to be the proper thing to do or consider but can negatively affect your personal productivity.

An example here might be the "cluttered-desk paradox," in which you leave things on your desk so that you won't forget them. Then they either get lost or, as intended, attract attention every time they are seen, thus providing continual distractions from whatever you should be doing. It's the good intention of leaving important stuff out that creates the paradox of having a distraction, no clean work space, and always having to look for something, thus the paradox. Sidebar 7.2 provides a list of other paradoxes that you might encounter.

TIME ROBBERS

Another area of personal productivity that requires attention in order to be controlled or eliminated are time robbers or time wasters. In her article "Time Management for Library Professionals," Lisa Peterson (1997) identified the top time wasters in various library settings. Items such as personal crises, lack of clear directions, meetings, and trying to do too much at once all ranked highly. And like a paradox, it is important to identify the causes of time robbers in order to determine a solution or fix the issue. Table 7.1 identifies common time robbers, the possible cause, and suggests a solution for each. These time robbers are general suggestions on self-identifying who or what causes you to become frustrated with the demands being made on your time and how you can work to improve your productivity and job satisfaction.

The reason this chapter is included in the book is because the very nature of community college libraries produces time-challenged librarians and staff. It is typical for a huge demand from random sources to dominate a typical day working in a

Table 7.1   Time Robbers

TIME ROBBER	POSSIBLE CAUSES	SOLUTIONS
Reading	Information overload	Read selectively; learn speed reading.
Too many details	Need to delegate	Learn and value principles of delegation and its benefit.
	Lack of priorities	Set and concentrate on goals.
Visitor interruptions	Enjoyment of socialization	Do it elsewhere; direct it to lunch or after hours.
	Inability to say no	Screen visitors, become unavailable to complete important task.
Indecision	Lack of confidence in the facts	Improve procedures related to fact-finding and validating information.
	Fear of making mistakes	Learn to embrace mistakes as a learning opportunity.
	Lack of a rational decision-making process	Get facts, set goals, investigate alternatives, implement.
Meetings	Overcommunication	Meet only if needed.
	Poor leadership	Use agendas; stick to topics needed; prepare minutes afterward.
Management by crisis	Unrealistic time expectations	Allow more time for problem solving or unanticipated issues to arise.
Lack of planning	Failure to see benefit of planning	Learn to recognize that investment of planning gains time and productivity later.
	Action-oriented style	Focus on results, not hard work or quick action.
Overcommitment	Broad interests	Learn to focus and say no.
	Confusion in priorities	Clarify priority expectations with supervisor.
Haste	Impatience with details	Slow down; get it right; save the time it would take do to again.
	Responding to the urgent	Distinguish between urgent and important.
	Trying to do too much in too little time	Attempt less; delegate more.

community college library. Knowing how to manage yourself, assessing how you spend your time, and working to improve the paradoxes and robbers that can cause you problems are critical to achieving success and feeling a sense of accomplishment; and there are other tips as well to staying organized and in control. For example, desk management is creating desk space for A, B, and C priority correspondence so you can manage accordingly. Then you address your A priorities first, etc.

Another thing about paperwork (it's here to stay): Handle it once. Skim it, mark it, act on it, delegate, discard, or Do It Now, but keep it moving. Managing your time includes how you file and keep correspondence for future reference by having it organized and readily available. Files should follow the 80/20 rule or use a color-coding schematic or have dead file dates. Also, use the same file name for paper and electronic files for easy retrieval.

Another technique in managing yourself is learning to prioritize each day but also to anticipate surprises or unexpected activities. For example, with prioritizing, line up a typical day in a "to-do" format, including common or routine tasks and activities. Chart out your day in relationship to other events, and know what's on your boss's to-do list as well. Then anticipate the surprises knowing that each day will bring exceptions. Be prepared to adjust your to-do list with each surprise. Don't let the surprises dominate the day, but be prepared to make drastic changes. Other tips to consider:

- Find and introduce, creatively, different ways of doing things.

- Manage your e-mails and phone calls—don't let them manage you.

- Challenge your own tendency to say "yes" without scrutinizing the request. Start asking and probing what's involved—find out what the real expectations and needs are.

- Think carefully about how you currently spend your time.

- Challenge anything that could be wasting time and effort, particularly habitual tasks, meetings, and reports where responsibility is inherited or handed down from above.

- Don't be a slave to a senseless process or system.

- Plan for preparation and creative thinking time in your daily activities, for the long-term jobs or projects, to break down the largeness of the task.

- Recondition others' expectations of your availability and their claim on your time.

- Keep a clean desk and well-organized systems.

When discussing priorities it is appropriate to refer to Stephen Covey's Time Management Matrix, in which he distinguishes between important and urgent activities (1999). This is critical to good time management within the library, especially as it related to group actions. Library staff should have a clear understanding of what things are considered important and what things are considered urgent, and how to recognize the difference. In his book *Put First Things First*, Covey recommends the following actions as they relate to important and urgent:

- Important/urgent—*Do Now*
- Important/not urgent—*Plan To Do*
- Not important/appear urgent—*Reject*
- Not important/not urgent—*Resist and Cease*

This can be a good rule of thumb in a dynamic, action-oriented environment, and it helps keep everyone focused and on the same page.

PROJECT MANAGEMENT

Many community college librarians are faced with projects that go beyond the normal daily activities associated with running the library. This can include building renovations or modifications, equipment or system changes, institutional demands of programming or shared activities with other departments, or projects that occur occasionally such as accreditation activities or program reviews. For that reason, it is important to look at project management in this chapter, as those skills differ from routine activities.

According to the Project Management Institute, a project is a temporary endeavor to create a particular result or a unique product or service. This means it has a definite beginning and end with specific goals and objectives. This doesn't mean that it will always be a high-level activity, such as a building renovation or an accreditation visit. It can also be self-initiated by the library in order to move forward on a particular issue. An example of this might be a weeding project that becomes necessary in order to make room for newer or more relevant books and materials.

So project management becomes the application of knowledge, skills, and techniques related to project activities to meet the objective. This includes the use of tools and resources, and all this should be purposefully directed in order to achieve success. The core activities of managing a project include:

- Identifying the requirements, typically the project scope, time line, and estimated cost
- Establishing clear and achievable objectives
- Balancing demand for quality, scope, time, and cost as they compete for attention
- Recognizing and adapting to stakeholder concerns and expectations

Above all, communication becomes key to avoiding pitfalls, delays, or persons upset with how things are going. Communicating to everyone what's going on and with detail is critical. The following tips on project management are adapted from *A Guide to the Project Management Body of Knowledge* (Project Management Institute 2004) so that they apply more specifically to a community college library environment.

Planning activities are the backbone of the project and will ensure that goals and objectives are met. There are many different books of tips that can help you (see, e.g., Kemp 2005). The most important tip is to do the *right* project. You must select one that gives you the strongest value for the money and effort spent. It must be appropriately aligned to your institution's strategic plan and provide a basis for going forward into the future.

A second important idea is to define the scope of the project in a clear and concise plan. If you don't have clear target goals, you can easily go astray. The plan should also include the entire project with enough details on how it affects services and staff. It should use visuals whenever possible. Working with pictures and words helps to bring people from different perspectives together so that they can all contribute to the successful end to the project.

Pick the right team of people who support and understand what needs to be accomplished. Break down the work plan and tasks so you can define the skills needed and match the people with those needs. Be honest with yourself and your team when there are gaps, and fill them with temporary hires or take the time to learn how to do it right.

Hire an expert when needed, and make sure that he or she fits your project. Just because a mover can move furniture does not mean they know how to move books. Every project is unique, and experts can help design a project to be done right the first time. Remember, your home institution has resources that can be utilized as well; sometimes you just have to ask.

There are nine areas that need to be considered in planning and preparing:

- *Scope*. Must be defined clearly, including cost considerations.
- *Time*. Must be unbiased and use accurate estimation techniques. Set up systems to gather, track, and analyze how time is going to be spent.
- *Quality*. Trace requirements and test throughout the project to reduce errors. Evaluate and include customers/patrons in testing, and remember that the goals are ultimately to improve customer satisfaction items and to add value to the organization.
- *Risk*. Plan for uncertainty; prepare for the unexpected. Perform "what ifs" of risk management with your team every week of the project.
- *Human resources*. Help each team member step up in self-management and technical expertise.
- *Procurement*. Get the supplies and resources you need. If your project involves contracts that have been negotiated by your home institution, ask for copies so that you have a clear understanding of expectations.
- *Communications*. Have a communications plan, and follow it so that you are in touch with all stakeholders throughout the project.
- *Integration*. Constantly direct corrective action. Evaluate all events that could change the project schedule

Keep the project on track with stages and milestones:

- Recognize accomplishments. Develop milestones to demonstrate accomplishments along the way.
- Every milestone is an evaluation of progress. If a project can't deliver value, be willing to cancel it.

Use feedback with your team, and focus on scope and quality in the doing stage:

- Teach staff to stay focused and on schedule; ensure delivery of milestones; manage project risk; and manage project change.
- Focus on scope and quality. Get it all done, and get each piece done right.

Follow through to success:

- Make sure that the benefits of a completed project are celebrated and shared with all involved. Use every success and every error as a chance to learn to do a better job.

- Compile project historical information and lessons learned to make future projects easier.

MANAGING MEETINGS

Earlier it was mentioned that one of the biggest wastes of someone's time can be meetings. In fact, a lot of literature addresses how the concept of meetings has become inefficient and unproductive, especially with technology that can support communication without everyone being in the same room. However, meetings do serve a purpose and can be important when used effectively. Good meeting management has four simple core elements: preparation, start, execution, and close with follow-up.

A good meeting must start with good preparation. This means a clear purpose, a detailed agenda that identifies anyone with a responsibility and any resources available that will be needed. Sending agendas out in advance also allows people to come to the meeting prepared for the discussion and with any relevant information. The right people should be in attendance so that delays aren't encountered waiting for information or approvals.

Meetings should be started on time, out of respect for those who were on time, and ground rules established as to behaviors and decorum. Good ground rules include time limits for speaking, no disruptive side comments or cell phone conversations, and a willingness to remain open to hearing the opinions of others.

Meetings should be managed and focused so that the outcome will be some form of productivity. This usually is finding agreement over decisions to be made or shared information, but it takes thoughtful decision making, constructive conflict, and participation by everyone involved. Issues that are tangential to the topic, or need to be referred to later, should be written on a flip chart or wipe board to address later in order to move the meeting forward.

The close of a meeting can be just as important, as this is where you check for understanding of decisions made, people responsible, and actions agreed upon. These should be clarified, reviewed, and summarized later to ensure proper follow-up by the appropriate persons. Acknowledging participants' contributions and celebrating achievements are part of ending a meeting with a positive outlook.

MAKING YOUR EMOTIONS WORK FOR YOU

Many books, articles, and presentations have been created and delivered on emotional intelligence since Daniel Goleman first wrote about it in 1995 in his book *Emotional Intelligence*, and emotional intelligence in the workplace has been studied and proven to be effective in creating a positive influence in a working environment. Emotional intelligence is a hidden advantage (Cooper 1997) and, properly managed, can drive trust, loyalty, and commitment. It also creates one of the best productivity gains by managing emotions over rational thought. More recently, emotional intelligence has been defined as appropriately calling upon information from the emotional center of the brain to be balanced with the information from the rational center of the brain (Sterrett 2000).

Due to the nature of work in a community college library, staff members already understand the rational information centers within their brains that help them perform the services needed or find the resources requested. But community college libraries are very dynamic and diverse in nature and require the emotional side of the brain to balance and support the rational side of the brain in order to be productive and successful. Community college librarians with high emotional intelligence would be equipped to handle just about anything.

So what is emotional intelligence, and how do you manage it? Emotional intelligence is characterized by a set of skills and competencies related to initiative, empathy, building trust and personal discipline. It includes the ability to cope with pressure in a variety of situations, and thus it is appropriate to include in this book.

The basics of emotional intelligence include knowing your feelings (self-awareness), managing your emotions (self-regulation), recognizing and having empathy for the emotions of others (social competence), and reacting appropriately to your emotions in relationship to others' emotions (building relationships). Most of us are emotional creatures, and communication is the physical aspect that links these skills together.

Being self-aware is important in many ways, but being self-aware of your emotions is the cornerstone for achieving emotional intelligence. This means that you can perceive your own emotions or how you feel within the moment during contact with others. This helps you to understand your tendencies or possible reactions given different situations. To do this effectively, you must be willing to tolerate the discomfort of negative feelings while being self-critical. That in itself is a strategy for improving your self-awareness: rather than avoiding a feeling, your goal should be to move the emotion, go further into it and eventually through it (Bradberry and Greaves 2009).

Another strategy for improving self-awareness, especially in a public services setting, is to learn who and what push your buttons, so to speak. By recognizing those particular people, situations, or events that cause an emotional response, you can learn how to manage that response effectively. Getting feedback from others is also important in broadening your perspective on how others perceive you when you feel a certain way. Being self-aware allows you to take actions and make decisions that will avoid negative interactions and help create positive ones.

When you are aware of your emotions, you are better equipped to manage or regulate them by understanding what will happen when you act or do not act. And not acting is a conscious decision as well if you are feeling avoidance or aloofness. Managing your emotions also helps you to stay flexible and direct your behavior into positive interactions. Strategies to learn self-regulation of emotions include speaking to someone who is not emotionally invested in the problem to once again gain perspective (Bradberry and Greaves 2009). Make a point to learn something from everyone you encounter; even librarians can learn something new each day.

Being socially aware to become socially competent is harder. This is learning to read and understand the emotions of others and recognize when their emotions or moods change. Part of why this is hard is because you have to perceive how other people are feeling, even if those feelings are different from you own. In a community college library, this can be critical because as a library staff member, you feel comfortable and knowledgeable about your environment, the resources available, and what to expect from the use of technology. Others coming into the library for the first time will not have that same confidence and will have different emotions from your own. This means that their reactions to things, people, and you will be different.

Using your social awareness skills to manage feelings and emotions that are different from your own is one of the emotional intelligence goals. This can reflect a positive communication exchange as opposed to a negative one that is emotionally charged. Demonstrated empathy toward others will reduce conflict and produce satisfying relationships. That is another strategy for building relationship skills: learn to value all types of people and relationships with them in order to learn from them as well.

HAVING THE CONVERSATION

David Lankes (2011), in his *Atlas of New Librarianship*, talks about the librarian's need to facilitate points of knowledge with different constituents as a means of improving society. In a community college, librarians and staff can certainly play an important role connecting people with knowledge to people seeking knowledge and advocating for the larger community. To do this, librarians and staff must be able to have those conversations and connect those areas of need with emotional constraint and maturity. As community colleges, their libraries, and user communities continue to evolve, learning to have the conversation becomes an important skill to master.

Many publications exist that try to identify and direct a skill set of communication in tough circumstances or situations. A conversation in such situations is deemed crucial or significant when the stakes are high, opinions vary on solutions or outcomes, and emotions run strong. Emotional intelligence skills can have a major impact on the way a conversation is conducted and can determine its effectiveness.

To draw comparisons, to be self-aware at the start is to recognize what motivations you have at stake and how they impact your discussion. This means you must decide how to be honest about the encounter by clarifying what you want or need from the exchange. Focus on the desired outcome—whether it's discussing performance or behavior problems, advocating for funding, recommending a particular resource, or instructing on a procedure—and know what the final result should be.

Self-regulate conversations by developing your points of view into stories that can be shared and that will help explain why you are taking a particular stand. Use of facts and accuracy will make a difference in developing a convincing argument. Be willing to listen, learn, and watch for the emotional reaction of others before responding to differing points of view. Finally, when having those conversations, make it safe for those who could feel threatened. Backing someone into a corner will not help meet objectives amiably but will leave emotional damage that will require correcting sometime in the future. Using your emotional intelligence skills to have productive and satisfying conversations is an important skill for maintaining integrity and credibility.

LEARNING TO CHANGE

Part of managing oneself is learning to change and helping others to do so as well. Change occurs when something transforms or is converted to something else. People generally don't like to change and will always look for reasons not to.

Change also takes resources or redistributes resources to other areas. In a business setting, this is necessary when sales decline, so some familiar business slogans might say, "Keep the machines in your factory but change what they do," or "Keep your customers but change what you sell." In libraries, the focus on change is different but could be similar conceptually. For example, "Keep your staff but change what they do," or "Keep your mission but change the scale or process." People's emotional sides need help or leadership to make the connection that change will happen, but if someone changes as well, all can be good again.

Personal change is a complex and sometimes difficult process to endure. John Fisher's *Personal Transition Curve* has been revised again in 2012 to include these stages that individuals can go through in affecting change:

- *Anxiety*—awareness of events outside of the individual's control
- *Happiness*—mimics excitement that something new or different is happening
- *Fear*—over an unknown change that may occur
- *Threat*—the implication that change will have an impact on how an individual perceives himself
- *Guilt*—comes when the implied fears and threats are reduced from heightened expectations
- *Depression*—recognition that past actions or behaviors do not work with impending changes
- *Gradual acceptance*—the changes are beginning to make sense within one's personal realm
- *Moving forward*—person exerts more control of situation
- *Disillusionment*—awareness that values, beliefs, and goals don't match changes
- *Hostility*—toward these changes and the effect of social failures
- *Denial*—lack of acceptance or acknowledgment of impact on self
- *Anger*—over the forced nature of a change or lack of control
- *Complacency*—changes were survived and events rationalized

It's important here to identify the emotional intelligence skills that can assist you as an individual in moving through changes so that you can then influence others. With changes that are occurring in higher education and even more dynamic changes occurring within community college institutions, changes can be expected to happen on an ongoing basis.

Paula Warnken's (2004) article on managing technology in libraries discusses change and how it is influenced by technology, among other things. In the study she conducted and with the experts she interviewed, the value and benefits of change are put in the context of being worth the effort it took to get there. She also identified these principles that were considered important to the success:

- Everything is connected to everything else, so think comprehensively instead of in a piecemeal manner.
- There is no one recipe for successful institutional planning. Start where you can get the most leverage, harnessing the leadership most likely to succeed and recognizing that change begets change in part because the institutional culture begins to change.

- Design a planning process that is clear and explicit but at the same time flexible and patient.
- Design a process that is inclusive, connects visibly with the governance structure in place, and overrepresents faculty and deans.
- Staff the process with competent, respected individuals who have the time to dedicate their full attention to the task.
- Prepare the institution for change by consciously fostering an expectation that change can directly improve the lives of faculty and staff.
- Learn from the experiences of others; there is no need to reinvent the wheel; use the planning process to strengthen a sense of community by clarifying values and vision.
- Integrate academic and financial planning, and use targeted fund-raising to support change.
- Communicate as often as you can, using multiple channels and strategies to reach all parts of the community at every stage of the process.
- Anticipate and mitigate major barriers to change by building transitional safety nets under major curricular or budgetary transformations.
- Involve the right outside consultants at the right time to break political logjams or to add expertise.
- Give change a chance; be open to fortuitous situations, and remember that there is no shame in taking advantage of good luck.

These principles can certainly be applied to needed changes within a community college library environment and provide some framework for embracing change by the entire organization.

In their book *Change the Culture, Change the Game*, Connors and Smith advocate that real change occurs when the culture itself changes through strong and clear leadership that has provided a direction for change (2011). People must be accountable, at every level, for lasting change to have the greatest effect on an organization. As for the larger organization, John Kotter's eight steps of transforming changes include establishing a sense of urgency; forming a powerful guiding coalition; creating a vision; communicating the vision; empowering others to act on the vision; planning for and creating short-term wins; consolidating improvements and producing still more change; and institutionalizing new approaches (1995).

DEVELOPING LEADERSHIP

The better you are at being self-managed, the better equipped you are to become a leader, if not in an official position, at least in status with others that you influence. Earlier your emotional intelligence was discussed as important for managing yourself and your relationships, and that manifests itself in your leadership ability. While IQ and technical skills are important, the skills present with good emotional intelligence traits can help position someone to be a more influential leader. In a community college library, a very dynamic and diverse environment, emotional intelligence skills can be critical.

Daniel Goleman's work on emotional intelligence (1999) began by studying competency models for various types of work. Then he applied the emotional intelligence principles to those competencies to see which competencies were impacted by emotional intelligence traits. Needless to say, any competence or related performance to those competencies can be improved with the proper use of emotional intelligence skills. The same principle applies to the competencies discussed in chapter 2 as it relates to a community college environment.

In his chapter "What Makes a Leader," Goleman goes on to match leadership traits to the emotional intelligence components. He supposes that a person demonstrating superior self-awareness skills can in turn influence the larger organization to be more self-aware in its decision-making or service processes. People who are good self-regulators create an environment of trust and fairness that encourage good behaviors from others involved in the work or activities.

Leaders are also good motivators whose reasoning and drive go beyond the confines of the job or tasks involved. Motivation doesn't have to come from a supervisor or manager; anyone can motivate or be motivated by demonstrating a strong optimistic attitude and a desire to achieve results. Likewise, the use of empathy (sensing and feeling emotions of others) is an important skill to master as we become increasingly team focused and depend on the talents of others to accomplish goals and objectives.

Finally, the ability to build relationships can be significant in demonstrating leadership and helping the organization find support systems. The development of social skills is not just about being friendly; it's about directing those positive feelings into other relationships in order to make connections and manage social situations. Goleman feels that emotional intelligence skills can be learned but must be purposefully identified and practiced in order to be effective.

MY STORY

As a retail manager, I was also a training manager for most of my career. Coming into a community college environment allowed me to reexperience training by sharing where I'd come from and how my experiences were useful in an academic setting. It was a very worthwhile experience, and I continue to share today.

FINAL WORDS

If life is nothing else, it's about managing yourself. Following the principles of emotional intelligence and being aware of your emotions and actions is one of the most important things you can do for yourself no matter what profession you belong to. Following time management or project management principles will not only make you more efficient but also give you a better sense of self-worth.

8

⸻•⸻

PLACE, BUDGETING, AND FACILITIES

Much of what happens in a community college library will be targeted to library staff to be integrated into its process. Across the country, operational models for community colleges and their libraries will vary, and the degree of support will change based on many factors, but primarily whether or not the campus and library are operating centrally or if functions are decentralized. This chapter discusses general issues related to facilities, budgeting, human resource management, and other operational issues that may or may not be the responsibility of any given library but do need an awareness from library leaders as to how these issues affect fulfilling the library's mission.

LIBRARY AS PLACE

Community college libraries can be many things to a very broad range of constituents. To name a few, they are "centers for information," or a go-to place when someone doesn't know where to find the answer. A common issue in community college librarians is that they are being asked for information beyond their normal scope of operation with an expectation that they will know the answer. Libraries can also be a haven for learners who need a special environment for inspiration, or are collectors of special items that are unique to a campus or community. This can include being a repository for archives and government documents, even locally based on the community need. The community college library is also a gathering spot for students and a visual anchor on campus; many community colleges offer few venues for group interaction, and the library becomes a logical choice. And so the library becomes many things to many people with different interests and demographics.

Identifying users can be important in making decisions about the facility. For example, a large user group would be undergraduate students, but they could also be divided demographically into students just out of high school and adults returning to school for additional education. Both of these groups would have

Sidebar 8.1 COMMUNITY COLLEGE LIBRARY SPACE ATTRIBUTES AND NEEDS

- Digitally literate
- Active, always plugged in
- Very mobile
- Communication oriented
- Learning from peers
- Not as private
- Want to be challenged
- Looking for instant gratification

different needs and expectations of the facility and library staff. Other user groups could include faculty who use library resources as part of the curriculum; community members who support the campus and expect to use the resources that they fund through taxes; and visitors, parents, or potential students who are investigating their future objectives or inspirations. Examples of needs are listed in Sidebar 8.1.

The library as a physical place becomes an important part of what the organization is and what it is expected to be. Within the physical building there is the expectation to promote learning, encourage achievement, crave knowledge, inspire creativity, provide scholarly resources, and preserve community work. Also, there could be an expectation to host cultural events and exhibits that promote community or academic inspirations. Once again, the library is expected to be many things to many different people.

Undergraduate activities account for a large part of the physical activities within a library facility. Undergrads, new to higher education, can have diverse attributes that are critical in space-planning activities. They are mobile and active, always plugged in and usually digitally literate. They are also communication oriented and not as private as previous generations. They want to be challenged but expect instant gratification. What does this mean for the facility? Group spaces are needed as well as plenty of infrastructure support such as electrical outlets and wireless; comfortable seating; food; and tools and equipment that promote collaborative learning. The library can combine central location, new technologies, traditional resources, group work space, computers, social spaces, user-focused support, and teaching spaces for this group.

Older adults returning to school might have different attributes or needs for the physical space. They typically are more private in nature, less comfortable working in open spaces or in groups, not as confident with emerging technologies and thus seek different types of space in which to do their work. These needs translate into more quiet spaces, individual carrels, or room options; access to traditional resources; and staff available for guidance or referrals. Other user types could have additional needs that should be identified and addressed in the management of space.

Camila Alire, in her book *Academic Librarianship*, discusses how library space on an academic campus is different than other spaces on campus. She lists three central reasons why library space must be considered in a different light, starting with "It's complicated." Library space combines space used for staff, users, collections, and teaching. To plan and make decisions on any one of these features without considering the others would be incorrect. This has been a problem with campus administration in the past when there was not a clear understanding of spaces needed for diverse activities and growth of collections and population.

This relates to the second reason, "Wear and tear," in which libraries endure a large amount of foot traffic from a variety of sources but do not always get a proportionate share of maintenance and upgrades. As a public space and one that is shared by a majority of campus users, the library should have priority on general building maintenance issues. That relates to a third reason, "Hours of operation." Most library buildings are in operation on any given day longer than other buildings on campus and thus warrant attention in this regard.

So library space should be considered an important part of the service and resource model that community college librarians present to their constituent base. This means that time and effort must be put into ongoing assessment of current use of space, and these assessments must include a user perspective, or else users will find other places to go. These assessments can be done with traditional assessment tools, and an important one is a formal observation study matched with meaningful attributes in order to get a sense of how space is really used. Paco Underhill, author of *Why We Buy* (1999), details the method of observation and its ability to impact retail and product space decision making.

Tangible data analysis is another way to assess your space and its use. Data such as gate counts, circulation stats, traffic trends, ILL requests, reference stats, and even facilities stats such as products consumed, energy used, etc., can be pulled together to both demonstrate the effect that the physical space has and help determine needs and efficiencies to be addressed.

A recent publication by Primary Research Group Inc. (2012) showed survey results regarding the redesign of library space including data obtained from community college library participants. The purpose of the survey was to develop trends about how librarians were investing in space redesign and to speak to trends of use of the space. To discuss library as a place, this list of space classifications from the survey might be useful:

- Collection space
- Electronic workstation space
- Multimedia workstation space
- Viewing rooms and listening rooms
- Space for special collections
- User seating space
- Staff work space
- Group work environments for patrons
- Storage space
- Auditorium or larger lecture space
- Museum or exhibition space
- Information commons

In addition to this list, library space rented to or otherwise dedicated to other college departments is also of consideration to the overall makeup of space and how users will use and interact within the given spaces.

The results of this survey are also interesting with regard to what is not happening. Of the community college librarians who responded to the survey, 64 percent indicate that capital spending on library facilities has remained unchanged over the last three years, and 100 percent indicated that no monies were being allocated to new or expanded buildings, this at a time when community college enrollment is up and library space is needed even more.

Other factors to consider when purposely designing library space include connectivity of common space attributes, how spaces connect together and transition, how to balance between different user groups, how to recognize shared spaces, and how to create an environment of respect. These factors come from staff support of space objectives, clear communication with a signage program, or the use of atmospherics to provide parameters and support of space objectives.

Library atmospherics can be important for many reasons. The concept is that environments create emotional responses in people and that this environment can be manipulated, such as in retail environments. This is important not only for creating the foundation for managing library space, but also in marketing of library services and influencing users' views of the library. Georgios A. Bakamitsos and George J. Siomkos, in their article "Context Effects in Marketing Practice" (2004), discuss how the affective state or mood affects presentation context and describe how this mood is then used to create attitude and behaviors.

Kolter (2001) describes atmospherics as the conscious designing of space to create certain effects, and Turley, Fugate, and Milliman (1990) state that atmospherics concerns the controllable items connected with the internal and external environment of a facility that elicit an emotional or physiological reaction. These can include things such as sights, sounds, and scents; how temperatures, noise, and lighting levels feel to users; and how pleasing both interior with furniture or colors and exterior, architecture, designs feel on a personal level. Other examples on the effect of atmospherics can include how a sign program is designed to meet multiple user types, or how displays are used to create visual excitement. How well staff members are informed and support these programs makes a difference as well. This checklist in Sidebar 8.2 covers the basics of atmospherics and the items you can consider.

Sidebar 8.2   ATMOSPHERICS CHECKLIST

BASIC CONDITIONS

- Basic housekeeping, clean, neat orderly (look at detail)
  - Waste cans empty
  - Tape residue, pencil/pen marks, etc.
  - Windows clean, door knobs clean/shiny
  - Floors, carpets vacuumed, hard surfaces swept, stains cleaned up

- Tops are clean and uncluttered (first line of vision)
  - Service desk, neat and organized
  - Bookcases, displays, magazine racks, etc., neat and organized
  - Signs and posters current
  - Directional information up-to-date and inviting

PASSIVE ATMOSPHERICS

- Static aspects of facility
  - Lighting, temperature, layout of stacks and computers
  - Permanent signage
  - Traffic patterns
  - Entrances (first impressions)
  - Textures (carpet, tile, metal, wood)

ACTIVE ATMOSPHERICS

- Interactive elements
  - Readings, events, lectures, programs, etc.
  - Exhibits and external contributions to the environment
  - Displays and the use of internal creativity to create *drama*

This conversation is included in this text because there are low-cost options that can be explored if appropriate or necessary. To make the best use of your library's space, a purposeful effort should be made. User groups should be assessed for their resource needs and habits, and existing space should be analyzed to determine flexible options, possible partnerships, and use of shared resources, with an eye to making the case for institutional support. Users will have different needs based on different circumstances, provide options for space use, not a one-size-fits-all approach.

The library as place is important for its role on campus. The library should hold a place of leadership within the campus physical structure by providing that dynamic and secure place for students, faculty, and staff to work and achieve personal goals of studying, learning, and reflecting. The library as an institution should also be a place to provide guidance to those unsure of where to go or who to engage. This role as it relates to diversity on campus can be significant. Users and their needs are changing constantly, and making a conscious effort to keep spaces up-to-date and relevant is an appropriate investment of time and effort.

EXHIBITS AND DISPLAYS

To provide some specifics on activities that can make a difference in the atmospherics or presentation standards within a library, a little discussion on exhibits and displays is warranted. These can be the best low-cost options available and just require being inviting and accessible. Exhibits can be requested, invited, or developed and should reflect a theme that is of interest to the patron base. Examples include traveling collections, local artists or organizations, academic departments wanting to promote, and community messages or memorials.

Mary Brown and Rebecca Power (2005) provide a great resource on the effective use of exhibits and how to address liability issues as well as keep track of borrowed or loaned items. They also address some of the policies that libraries should consider in order to maintain a consistent approach to other organizations that might seek library space for their exhibits. Their cataloging and policy recommendations are in Sidebar 8.3.

Sidebar 8.3   MAKING A CATALOGUE

Category information
- Object name or subject of the unit
- Reference to other units of similar topic
- Larger unit(s) this is part of

Unit information
- Type of work
- Title, if applicable
- Classification
- Description of the unit
- Parts of this unit
- Bibliographic reference, if appropriate
- Size
- Materials and techniques

Source information
- Donor/date
- Owner/contact information/date/conditions of loan
- Reference number
- Location information
- Loaned to/date (including contact information and conditions of loan)

Loan information
- Loaned to/contact information/date [to be] removed
- Conditions/expected return date/date returned

Other notations

EXHIBIT POLICES

- The purpose of having exhibits or a description of how exhibits help fulfill the library's overall mission.
- The spaces in your library available for exhibits.

- The duration or frequency of exhibits.
- The responsibility for exhibits.
- The procedures for reconsideration of exhibits (including an Exhibits Challenge Form).
- The criteria for exhibits.
- The exhibits application and scheduling procedures (including an Exhibit Application Form like the sample that follows).
- The rules and guidelines for exhibits.

From: Brown, Mary E., and Rebecca Power. *Exhibits in Libraries, A Practical Guide.* Jefferson, NC: McFarland, 2006.

Similarly, displays are usually in-house creations pulled from parts of the collection in order to tell a story or highlight a significant interest. When creating an in-house display, you should consider all the questions that revolve around that subject such as who, what, when, where, and why. Other factors to consider include color, balance or symmetry, emphasis, and proportion. The use of fixtures and equipment is an important component, and props are an excellent way to highlight a subject and are usually affordable.

A trend in recent years with regard to monograph processing has been to retain the book jackets on the books for the use intended. Publishers typically provide most monographs with a dust jacket to help protect it, but it also provides an informational role. The jacket can contain biographical information about the author, a publisher's summary, or art work that complements the book's theme or subject. These books with their jackets make great display options to provide colorful interest and excitement to the visualization of a library's collection.

Sidebar 8.4 shows a bookstore modelin which the jacket is used to promote the book for sale. Libraries can use this to create a sense of excitement or drama toward library holdings.

FACILITIES

Facilities on a community college campus typically concern three different areas. Design and construction are concerned with the building or modification of new spaces on campus or campus extensions. This is typically project work that connects

Sidebar 8.4 BOOK JACKET QUOTE

From Chip Kidd, famous book jacket designer: "book jackets give the book visual meaning."

A hardcover book is like a luxury item that appeals to a person's sense of belonging to the story. Good book jacket art helps a person make a connection with the story.

local and state building and fire codes to requests, needs, and ideas from campus administration. This is usually a component department of a larger facility operation and involves project work that is acquired through state and local procurement procedures. If you are considering a major modification to existing space, you will probably be directed to this group of people on your campus.

The next level of facility work is usually a facilities operation department that is in charge of maintaining existing buildings, grounds, and landscaping and the infrastructure needed to support a safe and secure environment. Typically, this is a centralized department that the library would contact for building repairs or equipment failures. Sometimes this includes the need for larger physical actions beyond what the library staff can comfortably accomplish. The key here is to be a partner with the facilities department on campus so that proper attention can be directed toward needed actionable items.

In most cases, housekeeping also falls under the facilities department but addresses the cleaning and more general maintenance of the campus and will usually have an established list of responsibilities. These responsibilities might seem limited, but they have been negotiated with administration so as to address expected costs and budgetary concerns, whether housekeeping is an in-house service or a contracted service from the outside. Once again, the key here is in knowing what is in the contract and being clear on the expectations of services provided.

Library staff members need to be prepared to address any facility issues that are not covered by the centralized institutional department. This might include housekeeping coverage at night or on the weekends, maintenance of library-specific equipment, or arrangements related to special events or outreach activities. Facility support will vary by institution, and it's important to be aware of what is available to you so that you can advocate.

BUDGETING

The budget process in community colleges will vary from state to state and even across different institutions within a state. For the purpose of this book, some conceptual knowledge will be provided, and the importance of budgeting will be emphasized. Everyone working in a community college library should recognize that budgets exist and have a purpose. A budget is necessary to forecast revenues and expenses in order to plan for cost-related actions.

Most academic budgets have a recurring base with the ability to make adjustments throughout the fiscal year. In most cases, budgets are centralized, meaning they are managed by the institution's accounting office and the library is working within the guidelines established by that office. Depending upon how the organizational structure is integrated into the budget process, the librarian may or may not see items such as payroll or shared costs for equipment or contracts that the college pays directly.

Librarians will typically be concerned with funding that comes from the allocation or portion provided by the institution, which is usually tax based on state or local tax measures. Also, opportunities are available to seek and, if successful, use grant funding for specific needs. These are usually project based and time limited. Finally, some libraries have the good fortune to have been endowed with monies from donors who will usually stipulate approved spending actions.

The majority of budget monies allocated to a community college library is spent on purchasing materials or licensing content for resources to support the academic curriculum. This is discussed in more detail regarding collection development and can include a variety of scenarios. For example:

- Subscription renewals should be considered first and should be scrutinized with usage stats and inflationary costs as to their continuation.
- Allocations of part of their collection's budget is assigned to academic departments that may make selections based on curriculum components.
- Request lists are maintained of materials asked for but not owned by the library. This can also include trends on materials obtained through interlibrary loan.

SECURITY

The issue of security generally falls under several subclassifications such as personal security of staff and patrons, building security from vandalism or theft, and overall disaster planning for weather events or large-scale institutional issues like the more recent "active shooter" situations. Almost any community college institution is going to have campus responsibilities identified and communicated on a large scale, in terms of expectations for actions related to preparation of safety and disaster issues, behaviors and logistical concerns during an event and after in terms of cleanup or recovery. All of these initiatives might include other issues such as security of data and protection of assets, health concerns such as pandemic outbreaks, and possibly even consideration for methods to continue services in the event of disruption to campus facilities.

Because community college libraries are all different with respect to physical demographics, relationships to campus administration, and potential threatening circumstances, a basic awareness of safety and security issues is needed, localized to each library's circumstances. The first priority is to have a clear understanding of the home institution's processes, expectations, and abilities to perform in a potentially problematic situation. From that framework, other considerations could be developed for the library specifically and communicated to staff, patron, and campus representatives as appropriate.

In June 2010, the committee on Safety and Security of Library Buildings from ALA's Library Leadership and Management Association (LLAMA) published an updated set of guidelines regarding library security: www.ala.org/llama/sites/ala .org.llama/files/content/publications/LibrarySecurityGuide.pdf.

These guidelines provide a basic look at building security issues and could be used to evaluate any given situation in order to determine if a library is meeting its needs in providing security. An example might be camera systems; if a library has one, is it sufficient? Or if not, do they need to consider investing in one?

Another useful resource, Miriam B. Kahn's *The Library Security and Safety Guide to Prevention, Planning, and Response*, has been updated and includes checklists and forms that can be adapted to any given set of circumstances (2008). The book covers public library situations as well and includes a section on staff responsibilities with regard to their safety and patron safety. This section can apply to a community college library especially with a large number of community patrons such as children. Once again, training and preparing staff for safety and security issues is one of the most important aspects of being prepared. Make sure your campus officials are in the loop so they know what to expect from you.

Kahn also has good ideas for protecting collections, and she segments how to handle different types of collections. A community college needs to identify any materials that are not replaceable in order to give this priority in the event of a disaster; or at the very least have materials of value documented with photos or lists so that items at risk will be known later.

A final resource to consider is Warren Graham's *The Black Belt Librarian.* Graham focuses on the people aspect of keeping a building secure, including managing patron behavioral issues (2012). He discusses staff training on how to handle problems and how to interact with third-party interventions such as campus police or security. In other words, you don't just turn a problem over to them; you need to have interaction in the situation.

In a community college library, student behaviors can have a disruptive effect on the overall mood and esthetics of the library and have to be addressed. In fact, one of the authors wrote about this in 2008. Crumpton's article "Sounding Off about Noise" addresses the noise issue that can be common in a community college library and offers suggestions to manage.

Safety and security must be an element of the operation that is proactively planned, communicated broadly, and reacted to effectively when a problem occurs. Such activities must be coordinated with your campus officials and customized to each organization's need.

MY STORY

Part of my retail experience was with a chain bookstore company. Many of the principles related to merchandising also apply to having a facility that is exciting and fun, thus the use of atmospherics in the workplace. Libraries traditionally have not employed some of the techniques retailers use to sell books, but with a clean facility and not much money, you can have a colorful and interesting point of view to show your patrons.

FINAL WORDS

Having your library clean and properly maintained is important, as well as staying within a budget and managing any human resources issues that might occur. Most community college libraries are going to operate in a centralized environment in which campus departments play a large role. It is important to see these roles as partnerships in order to work collaboratively in inspiring a strong, positive public perception.

9

COLLECTION DEVELOPMENT

In the 1980s, there was a general move toward naming community and technical college collections *learning resource centers* (LRCs) rather than libraries. With that name change, librarians could promote their collections as supportive of learning and indicate that they housed more than books. Collecting videos, slide shows, and interactive computer-based learning software was, in part, to acknowledge the fact that students had differing learning styles that needed to be satisfied with something other than print. University libraries were much slower to acknowledge these other formats (Bock 1984).

Community colleges did not always have library collections. Until the 1960s, the fledgling community colleges were often a corollary to the public education system and often used local high school or public libraries to serve student needs (Bock 1984). As community colleges proliferated from the 1960s to the present, their collections increased but relied primarily on textbooks as sources. Collections have continued to grow and diversify since then and now incorporate unique materials such as government documents, college archives, and even institutional repositories. In this chapter, collection management is examined as a broad set of activities including collection development, organization, assessment, and maintenance.

The purpose of a collection has been beautifully described by David Carr in an article entitled "A Community Mind" (2002). He writes that a librarian's highest task is to provide a way for our users to connect to their deepest thinking and to go beyond the curriculum and engage in free inquiry and lifelong learning. A passionately selected collection can allow community members to find themselves in the collected stories. Community colleges reflect the community story through what has already been written in books, journals, and videos. You can go beyond mere reflection into the creative story of our institutions in archival collections and can show the scholarly activity of faculty and staff in an institutional repository or collect the history of our region for the public to use.

According to Carr (2002), librarians must also provide public spaces for the alchemy of transformative learning to happen. As noted in chapter 5, information literacy is also about presentation, so a knowledge commons helps people to interact with resources. No library is more powerfully called to fulfill this need than a community college library. This chapter will show how that might be accomplished.

COLLECTING

In the *Standards for Libraries in Higher Education* (ACRL 2012, the library collection is covered by Standard 5, which basically states that a library should have the correct materials to support the institutional mission. The generality of this statement lies in stark contrast to the *Standards for Community, Junior, and Technical College Learning Resources Programs*, which were promulgated in 1990 and focused directly on the community college environment, and were much more prescriptive. In 1990, Standard 6, which covered collections, even included a table that related numbers of students to the desirable size of the book, serials, and video or film collection.

Still, the standards do provide a general outline that guides librarians in their collection work. Table 9.1 paraphrases the standards and indicates what parts of collection work will be affected by that standard.

The new standards encourage librarians to understand the unique requirements of the institutions that they serve and create the collections that meet the needs of their users. The standards do not give librarians leverage for a certain size of collection or the amount of money that must be spent. Instead, librarians must use assessment and advocacy to build a case for what the learning resource center collection should be. That case is more difficult in community colleges because there is no sense that the library collection is the heart of the institution as many believe to be true in older, more established universities. Community college collections serve a different purpose. They are focused on a wider variety of topics, they are built primarily to support the current curriculum, and they rely more heavily on a smaller number of more recent materials.

Without prescriptive standards to rely on for justification, learning resource centers must have clear policies that describe their collection and how it supports the

Table 9.1 The ACRL Collection Standards and Their Impact on Community Colleges (Adapted from ACRL with permission)

ACRL Standard	Collection Impacts
5.1 Reflect institutional focus of research or curriculum	General collection must reflect needs of academic subjects and diverse user communities
5.2 Formats that are accessible virtually and physically	E-resources and digitization
5.3 Unique materials	Institutional repository, archives
5.4 Appropriate infrastructure	Appropriate computer connections, buildings, and furnishings
5.5 User education on scholarly communication	E-textbook movement
5.6 Long-term access to the scholarly and cultural record	Focus on unique materials.

Used by permission of the Association for College and Research Libraries

Sidebar 9.1 COLLECTION MANAGEMENT POLICY

1. Overview
Mission and goals
Service communities
Subjects collected

2. Details of subjects, formats, and level of material
Include a description of the present collection, holdings, list of serials, and major reference works. Should include all formats.

3. Personnel involved in collections by job title
Should include a description of work with faculty, how a faculty committee is selected and functions, and responsibility of the selectors.

4. Gifts
What will be accepted and a clear statement that donated materials will be kept at the discretion of the subject librarian

5. Assessment

6. Preservation

7. Deselection criteria and management of discards

8. Handling complaints about the collection

Adapted from: G. Edward Evans and Margaret Zarnosky Saponaro. *Developing Library Information Center Collections.* Westport, CT: Libraries Unlimited, 2005.

institution's mission, goals, and objectives. A clear and current collection management policy can provide guidance that will ensure the success of the library within institutional constraints. It can be used to educate newly hired librarians, to acquaint administrators with the purpose of the learning resource center, and to communicate with all users. Sidebar 9.1 details the basic sections of an ideal policy.

Collection building begins with a description of the communities that will use it. For all academic libraries, constituents include students, staff, and faculty of the institution. Librarians should know the demographics of their institution as noted in chapter 2. Community college libraries have a more diffuse mission because they are often an integral part of the communities that they serve. Most community colleges are funded by local and county governments, the state, and a very small part by the federal government and compete for attention and dollars with K-12 education. They often have larger collections than local public libraries and have more specialized subject content that can benefit their local communities. In addition, they are often located in underserved or rural areas; therefore, they serve the public in their local communities, which can affect their collection decisions. In fact, some communities have built dual-use libraries that serve as both community college libraries and public libraries. Though they rarely have integrated collections, the message of dual-use libraries is that community college libraries serve more than just their campus community.

A collection is more than resources on a particular topic. In addition to the topical orientation of the collection, librarians must consider special kinds of materials for their different user communities. In universities, the faculty is an important user group for the collection, and their research interests must be satisfied. Typically, community college faculty members are not required to do research, but they are often taking classes toward advanced degrees or participating on research teams. The learning resources center can be helpful by offering support services and providing some materials that fit both faculty interests and the curriculum.

The presence of fiction collections in libraries has often been questioned or seen as only a corollary of the English curriculum. However, many community college students have not been academically well prepared. Reading can often be one way to increase academic performance. In fact, popular fiction, science fiction, and graphic novels have all been shown to increase reading levels for those placed in remedial, developmental, and English Language Learning classes (National Endowment for the Arts 2007).

Material in languages other than English is often suggested for inclusion in community college collections; however, it should not be an add-on without context. Resources should definitely be purchased for languages that are taught in the college but not necessarily to reflect the original language of the students. Rather, good English as a Second Language (ESL), sometimes called English Language Learning (ELL), collections are a better use for limited funds. Books in this collection should be simply written but not childish and cover topics that are important to adults. Collaboration with ESL or ELL instructors is essential.

Collection building is about identifying, selecting, and then acquiring the materials that will be a part of the library. Collection management processes are often called technical services and involve librarians and staff members working as a team to complete the many required tasks. This section will look at those processes and talk about staffing for these library services.

Identifying

Before librarians can acquire materials, whether books, videos, audio, or journals, they must know that those materials exist. The latest trend in identifying materials is called patron-driven (PDA) or demand-driven acquisition (DDA). Using this method, librarians wait until their patrons ask for something, and then they acquire it using the fastest method possible. However, there is still room for anticipating user wants and needs and having a collection that is selected by a librarian and available when a patron enters the library or accesses the library's electronic materials.

Just-in-Time Purchasing and Publishing

Using interlibrary loan (ILL) data to do collection building was the first use of what is now known as demand-driven acquisitions (DDA) or patron-driven acquisition (PDA). Community college librarians must ask themselves why they should risk their small collections money on materials that will not be read. PDA systems monitor the searches on your catalog and automatically alert you that a certain book has been requested. As the editor of *College & Research Libraries*, Joseph Branin (2009) writes, libraries in the digital age should not be buying collections of noncirculating materials. Instead, requested materials can be acquired immediately in the most expeditious way. Even further, some larger libraries have Espresso Book Machines installed, where an e-book can be printed on demand and paid for by the patron, or put into circulation in the library and lent to the patron. Either way, only the books that are needed or wanted are placed into the collection.

The Open Access Movement has inspired faculty members to publish their own textbooks rather than rely on the commercial publishers. The ethics and feasibility of libraries purchasing these materials is a difficult topic.

Identifying forthcoming or newly published materials requires librarians to monitor the output of publishers in the topics that are important to the curriculum. For instance, if the college supports a welding curriculum, a librarian should be assigned to monitor the publications produced by the American Welding Society. Sales brochures, vendor displays at conferences, and ads in library literature are all important ways of keeping tabs on potential additions to the collection. Another way to be informed about new titles is to work with salespeople for the publishers, sometimes called jobbers, who will visit occasionally with titles and brochures that fit your past purchasing or identified subject areas. Also, the faculty should be consulted on a regular basis for suggested materials, with the caveat that the library is not aspiring to a research-level collection.

Librarians in larger libraries identify new materials through approval plans, but most community colleges do not have the money to set up such a system. An approval plan is usually constructed by using a classification scheme, such as Library of Congress, and whenever a title is published in a particular call number range, the library is alerted. The material is either sent automatically or the order is approved manually to be sent. Many statewide networks of community colleges have moved to a centralized purchasing system that can use this type of ordering process. Librarians in individual libraries should assess the impact of such a system on usage to be sure that the right materials are being acquired. Similar plans can be set up for electronic books. Blocks of books can be leased, and then if usage is high enough, the book is purchased by the library.

Selecting

The existence of material does not mean that it should be in the library's collection. The quality of that item, the fit for the collection, and the value of it should be assessed first. In order to make such an assessment, the librarian must look at review sources, check comparable collections, and be aware of the publisher's authority.

Reviewing sources can be found online at book vendors such as Amazon or Barnes & Noble (bn.com), but they should be read with skepticism because authors can write their own reviews under pseudonyms. References to published reviews in sources like *Booklist* or *School Library Journal* that are found online should be checked for authenticity in the named sources. Yankee Book Peddler/Baker & Taylor offers reviews through their selection tool, GOBI3, which is a database of all of the content they offer. They also offer a special community college service that promises to provide updates on new content releases. Other vendors such as Follett have similar tools.

Another indicator of quality is to note whether other libraries have collected that material. It is a good idea to create a list of colleges with comparable curricula and then check their collections for materials on that topic. A good tool for seeing multiple collections is OCLC's worldcat.org. You can create a wish list of materials there and then decide what should be purchased or what could be borrowed when needed.

Acquiring

Once selected, the materials must be purchased in some format and from some source. These two choices are deceptively simple because they actually involve a series of decisions that are not always as linear as some literature seems to suggest.

1. *Format*
   Will you purchase the e-book, the paperback, or the hardback book? Will you buy the DVD or connect to a streaming service to provide access to a video resource? This choice category is a delicate balancing procedure in which price is merely one of the considerations. Another major factor is the availability of technology for student use: Do they own a device that streams video or reads e-resources? Is the e-resource in more than one format? For example, is it accessible from both PC and Mac platforms? Does the average age of the students that you serve argue for one format over another, or do you need to have both? (See Sidebar 9.2 for more information on electronic resources.)

2. *Source*
   The next step is to choose a source. Do you buy from Amazon.com, from a general vendor such as Yankee Book Peddler/Baker & Taylor, or directly from the publisher? Because many community colleges are small-volume purchasers, direct purchase from a publisher can sometimes reduce costs, even though vendors offer discounts. One strong reason for using a major vendor is that cataloging records are available at the time of purchase. Investigating a source may lead to a different decision about format. So you have to allow for revisiting the decision that you made in step 1.

3. *Ownership vs. Access*
   Since the advent of full-text journal databases in the 1990s, librarians have struggled with whether to own content, primarily in paper, or simply to provide access to it as digital content. The Open Access Movement and developments like institutional repositories, the Google Book collection, and other digitized content have made that decision much more complex and difficult. Can a library exist with just free e-resources? Should a library pay for e-content? How much print material should you own? Certainly, the fate of print reference collections is a blueprint for what might be coming for owned print materials (Detmering and Sproles 2012; Francis 2012). As more and more encyclopedias, indexes, and other standard reference materials are presented as e-content, librarians struggle with the question of what their reference collection should be. The basic question is, should libraries provide only access to Wikipedia, or to the *Encyclopedia Britannica* online, or to the print version of *World Book*? Or is it better to choose all three? The same questions should be asked for the general collection.
   Access to materials involves paying recurring costs that are difficult for small libraries to bear. Providing access to web-based materials requires some technical knowledge including how to configure proxy servers, deal with off-campus users, and provide technical assistance as needed by users.

4. *Cooperative Arrangements vs. Single Purchaser*
   The advent of electronic materials made it much easier to share the cost of materials. Most databases, electronic reference sources, and e-books are

Sidebar 9.2 NOTES ON ELECTRONIC RESOURCES

In the past, the electronic portion of a collection was considered in a vacuum. Older introductions to collection management practices had special sections on e-resources. Now, e-resources must be considered alongside all other collection decisions. As noted in the Acquisition section, librarians must choose format, and e-resources require different management practices that involve cooperation with college IT departments or employment of a knowledgeable systems librarian. Issues that are part of e-resources include:

- *Licensing and Digital Rights Management (DRM)*
  - Because e-content is accessed and not owned, the content producers hold copyright and control rights to it. When you contract with a vendor, understand the limits of the license. Even though you are open to the public, you might not be able to offer use of particular resources to members of the community because of these licensing limitations. DRMs enforce the limits of what your users can do with content.

- *Assessment and Deselection*
  - Even e-resources need to be assessed for usefulness. Vendors can often supply statistics, but librarians need to determine what will count as use. Is it simple access? Or is the number of times downloaded a more important measure? Work with the vendor or the consortium supplier to develop good assessment measures. Deselect that tool or title when appropriate (Larson n.d.. E-resources use up cognitive space for users just as surely as books do shelf space.

- *Proxy Servers*
  - In order to access content from a noncampus location, students, faculty, and staff must be able to use a single login and acquire a campus IP address. This is managed by a proxy server. A library staff member should either manage this function or be a liaison between the IT department and the vendors because issues arise continuously.

purchased through consortial membership. Many states have set up statewide consortia that provide database access to all of the institutions in that state, for example. *NCLive* in North Carolina or *IConn* in Connecticut. Consortial pricing can also be obtained through regional OCLC networks, like Lyrasis. Membership in any consortium requires compromise. To save money, the consortium often works with a single database vendor like EBSCO, Proquest, or Gale/Cengage. This may not offer the right database mix for your particular constituents. Many libraries belong to more than one consortium to maximize their collection dollars.

Sharing collections on a deeper level is often called cooperative collection development (CCD). It is more than just deciding to share the costs of an expensive resource, like a database. It involves joint decision making about building collections in only one institution for the benefit of all. One library decides that they will collect in nanoscience, while the other concentrates on nanoengineering. When collections are shared at this level, then other sharing must follow, including shared borrowing arrangements and shared storage facilities if appropriate.

Processing

A wide variety of systems are used to track materials from acquisitions through cataloging and then into circulation systems. Integrated library systems (ILS) once required an investment in locally run hardware, software, and maintenance, or joining together in a multi-institution consortial system. Now, small libraries can run their own systems with generally available hardware and software. ILS systems will be discussed more thoroughly in the next chapter. For now, newly received nonelectronic materials must be marked "received" in the ordering system first. Then a catalog record must replace the "on order" record in the catalog. Finally, the item must have ownership marks put in place, a call number placed on the spine, and the book cover secured or discarded.

MANAGING

Once a collection has been acquired, management processes begin. The collection must first be organized, then conserved and preserved, and when it has come to its useful end, it must be deselected.

Organization

School and public libraries use the Dewey Decimal Classification (DDC) system to organize their collections, while academic libraries primarily use Library of Congress (LOC) classification. What should a community college library use? Some argue for DDC because it makes the transition from high school easier, while others point out that LOC is what community college students will use when they go on to the university level. This debate becomes a local issue in many cases.

Conservation and Preservation

Conservation is all of the processes that a librarian uses to prevent their collection from losses, while preservation is what is done when something has already happened to an item in the collection. Conservation includes policies that protect the collection, like prohibiting food, drinks, and other materials in the library. Other good conservation policies include temperature regulation, use of security devices, and training of staff in the proper handling of materials, especially student workers.

Preservation is not a major concern for community college libraries because currency is a more important consideration; however, preservation of unique materials should be considered. A policy governing what will undergo preservation processes such as repair, binding, and replacement of pages should be part of the collection management policy (see Sidebar 9.1).

Collection Assessment

An excellent example of a collections case study for a single library can be found in a chapter by Robert Kelly (2006), in *It's All about Student Learning: Managing*

Community and Other College Libraries in the 21st Century. For a statewide study of 28 Florida community colleges, Perrault et al. found that although libraries were adequately funded at the founding of the college, the same levels did not persist over time, leaving most schools in the study with outdated collections (1999). The authors recommend adding 5 percent new materials to the collection and withdrawing the same amount every year, something they termed the Continuous Update Model.

In order to implement the Continuous Update Model, libraries must have data about their collections. As Perrault et al. (1999) note, the data that they used for their study came from a statewide catalog and circulation system that all community colleges shared. Age of the collection, age of particular call number ranges, and item circulation can be retrieved from any circulation system. In a study of one college library, Debbie Dinkins found that only 25 to 34 percent of purchases accounted for 80 percent of the circulation, which confirms the basic 80/20 rule of collections.

One major impetus for collection evaluation is a change in the curriculum offerings at the college. Community colleges have especially volatile course and program offerings, as they are often mandated to respond to local workforce training needs and priorities. Accreditation requirements for some fields require that a library collection be a particular size and have specific materials available to students. It is essential that librarians be informed of pending curriculum changes, and the best way to achieve that is for the library director or other staff member to serve on whatever committee reviews change proposals.

Anne Marie Austenfeld (2009) outlines a comprehensive strategy for coping with new courses and programs in a small college environment. She recommends that college administrators set up a course and program approval process that requires the librarian's approval. Librarians should evaluate their own collection against at least one other school that is supporting the proposed program. Methods for doing so include using manual tools such as a review of Worldcat with topic searches or automated tools such as Worldcat's Collection Analysis module for larger projects (OCLC n.d.). Consortia partner collections should be examined for potential sharing. Journal and database recommendations should be scrutinized carefully, as these represent a long-term commitment for libraries. It is better to rely on interlibrary loan at the start of a program to assure sustainability for the long term before buying journal access.

Discontinued programs should also stimulate a review of the collection, since new acquisitions will not be necessary in that field and specialized journals can be put on the cancellation list. To paraphrase the famous Ranganathan (1957) statement that the library is an organism that grows: librarians must trim and weed their older collections as they obtain new ones.

Deselection or Storage

A number of studies have shown that libraries with more room on the shelves are better used by their users. Overcrowded shelves make finding the book you are seeking more difficult. Claire Fohl notes that this activity is less painful if there is a regular rotation through the collection; for instance, every second summer the focus is on science and the other summer the focus is the humanities (2002). Fohl goes on to describe an activity that includes librarians and faculty in joint decision making about what should be kept in the collection.

The CREW Manual (Larson n.d. is a wonderful blueprint for doing weeding. Identifying candidates for weeding is simple: choose a target age and a circulated-since date. For instance, you might identify all of the books older than 15 years and all those that have not circulated in the last 5 years. While that is just the first step, weeding should not be equated with simple discard but with the mirror image of selection. Although it can be time-consuming to choose, the result is a healthier collection that will serve users more efficiently. Recycling and reusing should be encouraged; sometimes librarians with other collections are eager to have what is no longer useful to you. Book sale tables to sell the books to people who come in the door or on eBay can be profitable occasionally (McGowan 2011). Do not let these activities prevent you from completing the real task, making room in your library for new materials and for users to interact with your collection.

Be careful to follow the proper procedures for disposal in your institution. Materials purchased with public monies can be treated like equipment and must go through special deaccessioning. In addition, make sure that you follow procedures for selling surplus materials. Some institutions do not like the library to keep that money.

UNIQUE COLLECTIONS

The future measure of a successful library collection will not be the size of the collection but the uniqueness of the materials that it gathers. With popular materials easy to access via the Internet, librarians must look to their communities to build collections that reflect their individual character. Archives, government documents, and special collections were once found only in large academic libraries, but some community colleges house these unique collections. The convergence of libraries, archives, and museums has happened in other sectors, such as public libraries, and the trend may continue into community colleges, as well.

Archives

The library may already be responsible for the archival function, but it is still fairly rare in community colleges. In addition to the responsibility to collect and organize the administrative productions of the college, the collection of student materials is also important. Bell and Gaston (2005 give a strong rationale for establishing an archives in the community college. Though the article reflects a unique aspect to the situation where historically black junior colleges were merged with majority white colleges in the 1960s, the importance of maintaining a sense of a school place in the community and in the lives of its alumni is an essential lesson for all librarians. Bell and Gaston describe the process they went through to gather memorabilia and documents that reflected the historical institution (2005.

The college yearbook is often a simple place to start an archival collection despite the fact that in many community colleges responsibility for such a publication lies in the highly dynamic hands of student groups. At Gateway Community College in New Haven, Connecticut, the yearbook was created by a student group that occasionally did not have members. The same problem prevents other student publications like newspapers and literary magazines from being consistently produced. Embarking on an archival program in the learning resource center requires that a staff member be designated to monitor the student groups and their output.

The problem is exacerbated in the digital age because many of these publications are now only created and distributed on the web. Archival programs must establish relationships with content producers and see if they can have a sustainable copy of the productions. A program with the Internet Archive might be a possibility. The North Carolina Digital Heritage Center sponsored a unique program that digitized yearbooks from colleges across the state. The Internet Archive loaned equipment and staffing and hosts the files on their servers. The Digital Heritage Center worked with schools to obtain the materials and supervised the digitization. (See North Carolina College and University Yearbooks for more information about this project.)

Local History and Museums

Gathering and reflecting the history of the school is important, but community colleges may also be a place where the local community can be served. Some librarians have taken the initiative to start and maintain collections that preserve the history of the area that they serve. One such collection is at the North Carolina Wilkes County Community College James Pardue Library, which has a local history collection of books, a local history YouTube channel with reminiscences of residents of the county, and the archives of a local poet. The local history was supported by a series of state grants to the library (personal communication).

The possession of three-dimensional objects in some libraries occasionally leads to the need for a museum presentation of parts of the collection. For instance, in Alamance Community College in North Carolina, there is a local history museum that was endowed by the family that donated the money for the establishment of the college. Other community colleges have small art collections that are managed by curators who report to the library director. Unique objects are sometimes given to the library as gifts.

Institutional Repositories

Institutional repositories are Internet-based collections of the scholarly output of an academic institution. They are part of the scholarly communication revolution that has occurred within the last decade with the advent of online, open-access journal publishing. It might be argued that two-year colleges do not produce "scholarly" information, but they do produce content that is unique to them. Reports from task forces, student projects, student publications, and faculty articles are all possible content that might be put in an institutional repository.

Most institutional repositories are built on open-source platforms like DSpace. Some platform providers like Berkeley Electronic Press are making it possible for institutions to participate without running their own installations. Under Berkeley's Digital Commons program, they will host conferences, journals, and even books. Other vendors offer similar opportunities.

Government Document Depositories

The Federal Depository Library Program (FDLP) was established to ensure that basic documents produced by the government were available throughout the United States. Each Congressional District is eligible to house a depository in some established library. Most depositories are large university libraries, but there are about two dozen located in community colleges. The FDLP distributes materials that are produced by the Government Printing Office at no cost to the library. It can include many desirable publications, such as economic reports, laws, and congressional hearings. A depository library must designate what percentage of the large number of print materials it will accept; a small library usually accepts about 10 percent. A community college must think about the cost in person hours that are incurred in managing such a collection; however, the designation can be prestigious and can supplement a low budget. A government documents collection can support the surrounding community by providing access, something that is often part of the primary mission of the college.

Special Collections

Most learning resource center librarians do not go out of their way to add rare books to their collections. However, sometimes they are given as gifts or have become important simply because they are not owned by other collections. Visser (2003) gives a succinct introduction to identifying and managing items that should be in a special collection. She notes that standards of the Rare Books and Manuscripts Section (RBMS) of the American Library Association have four criteria that should be considered to designate a rare item in the collection:

- Age—older than 1801
- Artifactual importance—signature by the author or rarity of the binding or edition
- Institutional strengths—renowned program in welding
- Condition—able to be preserved

Once identified as rare or special, the decision to maintain and preserve such items must be carefully considered. Are there enough staff time, knowledge, and resources to do it? It may be better to consider selling or donating them to a larger collection so that they can be properly managed.

Digitization of Materials

Once available only to large, rich collections, building a digital library from digitized materials has come within reach of small collections. The emphasis should be on unique materials and collaborative projects that bring together other institutions to build resources that will have an impact on the community. The digitization process can be done in-house but does require some expertise to do it correctly.

A more attractive option may be to outsource the digitization process and the digital collection hosting. Lyrasis, a former regional OCLC affiliate, now offers both of these solutions to libraries. Small projects may also be done by commercial firms, such as iMemories or MemoryHub, that are marketing their services to consumers as places to house pictures, video, and audio that they will convert and store. They do not produce a digital library, but the conversion to digital artifacts could form the basis for that service.

MY STORY—WEEDING STRENGTHENS THE COLLECTION

The shelves in my community college were black steel. They had been purchased from another library, and in a windowless room, they made the library seem very dark. The shelves were crowded with old materials; many of the books had been purchased from a defunct religious four-year college. Many books on theology and philosophy were not even taught at the college. One summer, my colleague insisted that we weed. We all had other things to do, and it wasn't a priority for me; but the number of books that we owned was misleading. You couldn't find the good parts of the collection for all of the old, inappropriate books that were there. So we weeded. The next year circulation rose. New books could be seen and appreciated. And the black shelves were replaced. The library was a happier place.

FINAL WORDS

Your collection reflects your community mind. It is more than the books and resources gathered from published sources. It is also about reflecting the kaleidoscope of your user groups. Some of these tools may not fit what you can accomplish alone, but think of banding together with institutions that can help build the tools that you need.

10

DIVERSITY CONSIDERATIONS

Community colleges developed to directly serve the communities in which they are located. To that end, they have created a broad vision of educational equity and maintain open enrollment policies that allow for the most diverse group of students to attend postsecondary education. A recent report for the American Association of Community Colleges (AACC) states as part of its introduction that the association's commitment to access and inclusion for every person is based on the core values of its member colleges (AACC 2011). As librarians who provide service to such diverse clients, you must be able to engage with each person as an individual. Understanding group characteristics can help to fashion services that work for each person.

Other chapters examined the demographics of community colleges and how they affect reference service, information literacy instruction, and collection development. This chapter will examine aspects of diversity in greater depth and then offer tools to help develop your connection with all library clients, faculty, and administrators. The last section will look at using ideas from organizational communication to build relationships that will help you promote the library as an essential service.

THE SCOPE OF DIVERSITY

For over a decade, there has been acknowledgment throughout the library profession that there is simply not enough diversity in the library workforce. Recent statistics reviewed by the American Library Association Office of Diversity confirm that less than 12 percent of librarians identify with a race or ethnicity other than white (American Library Association Office of Diversity 2012). Although this is a problem for all libraries, the incredibly diverse communities in a community college challenge librarians without special training in dealing with multicultural and multilingual environments.

An informal portrait of community college librarians can be garnered from an unpublished survey taken in 2010. The sample of 190 respondents revealed that the diversity in community colleges may be even lower than the ALA statistics as

97 percent of respondents chose White as a self-description. That poll also revealed that only 46 percent of the librarians knew another language other than English. In addition, most had been librarians for more than 25 years, indicating that they were close to 50 years of age. And finally, 81.3 percent of the respondents were female.

The average community college librarian is therefore white, female, English-speaking, and probably middle class by virtue of the job that she holds, characteristics that can distance her from the communities she hopes to serve. The possible communication gaps can be overcome if attention is paid to them. Many factors make up cultural diversity through the community college lens and may affect library service. The list is not exhaustive but meant to stimulate thinking about issues that might limit your effectiveness as a librarian.

Ethnicity and Race

When discussing diversity and libraries in the United States, race and ethnicity is the first topic that is mentioned. The long history of excluding racial minorities from educational institutions including libraries has highlighted its importance. In the past, race categories were fairly straightforward, including White, Black, American Indian, and Asian, but the checkboxes masked the complex reality that was being represented by these words. In the 2010 census, new demographic categories were used for the first time to better capture the nuances. Categories for more than one race were included, as was a separate counting of people who are white but have a Latino heritage. In any case, the ethnicity statistics in community colleges can be seen clearly using the American Association of Community Colleges interactive interface to the Integrated Postsecondary Education Data System (IPEDS) called Community College Enrollment (see the tool at http://www.aacc.nche.edu). The view can be changed to look at the demographics of community colleges in the entire country or in a particular state. The tool has charts for attendance status, that is, full-time or part-time, gender, and ethnicity. The ethnicity chart shows both racial and ethnic statistics.

Ethnicity is broader than race as a descriptor, and that has implications for library service. Even when students check off the box for White, they may come from an ethnic group that gives them a different view of what librarians do and how a library can help them. For instance, many new immigrants from Eastern Europe are more familiar with closed-stack arrangements in libraries. They may come to the service desk asking for your help in retrieving a book from the shelves. This simple request can lead to exasperation on the librarian's part and an unsatisfied and resentful library patron.

Refugees and Immigrants

Immigrants come to the United States voluntarily due to job relocations, joining families, or simply to try to better their circumstances. Most are here with documentation that allows them to study, work, and possibly apply for permanent residency. Undocumented immigrants and their children face special circumstances that play out in a hodgepodge of state regulations that affect each community college differently. Despite urging from organizations like the American Association of Community Colleges and the Community College Consortium for Immigrant Education (see their website at http://www.ccie.org) to create a national policy for immigrant education, regulations continue to be promulgated by states individually.

Refugees are immigrants who have fled their homelands due to war and dislocation. They have gained legal entry into the United States after living in refugee camps and resettle in communities where suitable services and opportunities exist by organizations like Lutheran Family Services and others. Today, major refugee communities are found in Greensboro, North Carolina; Seattle, Washington; Minneapolis-St. Paul, Minnesota; and Atlanta, Georgia. Although they share the same immigration status, refugee groups have unique needs; for instance, their countries of origin may not have had any libraries, so designing tours and instruction that introduce them to library systems is an essential part of their literacy education. Introducing the concept of free service, borrowed materials, and a range of resources can help students gain experience that will aid in their success in the content areas that they are studying.

Language Diversity

People from immigrant, refugee, and minority ethnic backgrounds often come to the community college to gain English-language proficiency. According to the Council for the Advancement of Adult Literacy (CAAL) report on adult ESL (Crandall and Sheppard 2004), extensive programs in English as a Second Language (ESL or sometimes ELL, English Language Learning are available in community colleges. The report distinguishes several different types of ESL students:

- *Generation 1.5 students*—Students whose parents do not speak English but who themselves were educated for some time in U.S. education.
- *International students*—Those who enter the United States and must reach English proficiency before entering full-time study.
- *World English-speaking students*—Students who were instructed in English in their home countries but have not reached proficiency in Standard American English. They need more practice with reading and writing.
- *ESL Literacy student*—Students who are not completely literate, that is, cannot read and write, in their native language.

Not included in the CAAL report was a term often encountered in the literature, limited English proficiency or LEP. For example, even though users may be able to express themselves in English in some domains, that does not mean that they understand the words used in psychology or medicine.

As noted in chapter 9, the resource collection can help promote general literacy for ESL students by offering properly chosen materials. Information literacy programs must be specially designed for these classes and might be tailored specifically for the groups outlined above. Generation 1.5 students may have only some information-seeking problems, while international students would have a much different set of issues with finding and using information resources.

Physical and Mental Health Challenges

Higher education has many issues with proper facilities for people with physical and mental ability differences. The Americans with Disabilities Act of 1990 requires

Sidebar 10.1   WE ARE ALL DISABLED

One of the most powerful cultural awareness experiences that I have had was at the Third Annual Access and Equity Conference at the University of North Carolina at Greensboro. The keynote speaker opened his talk with a simple statement that all of us will be disabled at some point. He reminded the audience that if they wear glasses, they are technically disabled. If they have trouble negotiating the stairs, they are not perfectly abled either. Even if we were perfect at this moment, he reminded us that did not mean that we would continue to be because old age, accidents, and illness may make us disabled in the future. How many of us have eyes that need glasses or contacts to fix? How many of us have had a broken limb that has required us to ask for assistance for even small activities like climbing the stairs? How many of us can reach the top shelves in the library stacks? We don't think of these as disabilities because they are temporary or easily corrected. Yet we are not perfect, and neither are the people we serve in the library. Their physical and mental challenges may be permanent, but they are still trying to get through their lives and deserve respect for overcoming the barriers that they face every day.

I will never forget Carlos, who was a work-study student in my community college. He used a wheelchair due to paraplegia caused by a fall from a roof. He rolled himself around obstacles in the library workroom without complaint; even though it was absurd that we could not move the book carts that were left in the aisles, or replace the chairs that where they should be, or properly place the trash cans. He also endured the lack of proper handicapped-accessible bathroom facilities in the entire college building, not just the library. His dedication to his studies and coming to work every day despite chronic pain caused by his condition was a lesson for me. Yes, we have all been disabled and may be again. We can learn to provide proper services for those who face these issues as a chronic condition.

better facilities, accommodations, and other services for people dealing with these issues. Facilities, especially, have been slow to be upgraded because of exemptions for government and nonprofit facilities (Willis 2012). If your facility has not been properly built, then the answer to these inequities is to provide service where the physical facilities are not welcoming. Make sure that wheelchair-bound students know that they can ask for assistance to reach items in the stacks and offer it when necessary. Other tips can be found on the website of the Association for Cooperative and Special Services (ASCLA), a division of the American Library Association, which is primarily aimed toward public libraries but can be useful to all library facilities. (See Sidebar 10.1 to read more about working with physical disabilities.)

Work toward changing the physical layout of your library to the proper specifications as the population of physically challenged adults will continue to grow from groups of returning Iraq and Afghanistan war veterans and improved health care for those with cerebral palsy and other physically limiting diseases.

Mental health issues are omnipresent on college campuses. Educate yourself about ways to be responsive to students in distress. Since libraries have more open hours than many other services on campus, they can be a site for impromptu counseling. Though a librarian can never replace a trained counselor, being prepared to deal with signs of struggle can help a student succeed in his academic work.

In addition, we can help by providing resources that could help students through difficulties. A collection of such books can also be helpful to students completing essays, presentations, or other assignments for English classes, so the expenditures are easily justified.

Learning Differences

Many people come to community college because they did not do well in or perhaps even dropped out of high school. Sometimes that lack of success can be attributed to differences in learning style. Recognition of that difference led to the expansion of libraries into learning resource centers in the 1980s.

Community colleges have a menu of options for furthering education that can fit students with a variety of academic challenges. North Carolina community colleges use the following language to describe the programs they offer. The language may differ from state to state, but the intention of these programs is often the same.

- *Adult Basic Education*—focuses on increasing facility with mathematics, reading, and language skills.
- *Adult High School*—full courses on topics that would have been taken in high school but revamped for adults.
- *Career Readiness*—a suite of classes focused on updated technology skills, language proficiency, and resume writing.
- *Compensatory Education*—designed for those with intellectual disabilities or traumatic brain injury.
- *General Education Development*—courses designed to help the student take the GED exam and have an equivalent to the high school diploma.
- *Skills Training*—focused on the acquisition of a particular skill such as machining. These programs are often geared to a particular employer or work setting.

Information literacy instruction and tours can be designed specifically for these different groups. A case can be made that information skills are at the heart of all of these programs. Gaining information literacy through instruction might be the best path to success for these students.

Gender and Sexual Orientation

The majority, 61 percent, of community college students are women. Although no variation in library services is implied by gender differences, it is important to note that many female students also fit the definition of nontraditional students: they are older, they have children, and they are returning to school after some absence. Librarians can help students to navigate their return to school by providing information resources that aid their reentry into the academic world.

Sexual orientation and gender identification are negotiated during young adulthood. While there are many traditional-aged 18–22-year-olds in the college community, many need to be informed about gay, lesbian, bisexual, and transgendered (GLBT) issues. Displays of information resources and special LibGuides can help students know that the library is a safe place to negotiate these identity issues (Hamer 2003).

Generational Differences

In 2002, the National Center for Educational Statistics *Condition of Education*, an annual report about all levels of education, defined a nontraditional student as one who had any of the following characteristics (Choy 2002):

- Delays enrollment (does not enter postsecondary education in the same calendar year that he or she finished high school);
- Attends part-time for at least part of the academic year;
- Works full-time (35 hours or more per week) while enrolled;
- Is considered financially independent for purposes of determining eligibility for financial aid
- Has dependents other than a spouse (usually children, but sometimes others);
- Is a single parent (either not married or married but separated and has dependents); or
- Does not have a high school diploma (completed high school with a GED or other high school completion certificate or did not finish high school).

The average age of a community college student is 29 years old, and two-thirds of community college students attend part-time. Therefore, a large number of community college students fit the NCES definition. Nontraditional students are often more motivated than their traditional-aged counterparts, but any of the listed characteristics might present barriers to success.

Another aspect of generational differences is that 42 percent of community college students are the first in their families to attend college (AACC 2012). According to Jeff Davis (2010), the number of first-generation students in community colleges will continue to increase due to immigration and birth patterns in the United States. Davis contends that first-generation college goers are much more likely to be challenged by the college culture and to lack persistence in college when they encounter barriers. Many colleges have instituted First Year Experience–type courses that can be an opportunity for the library to reach out to both nontraditional and first-generation students as they acculturate to this unfamiliar environment. Librarians can be an integral part of and even teach such a course.

RESPONDING TO THE CHALLENGE OF DIVERSITY

The American Library Association (ALA) has responded to the diversity challenge by trying to recruit more librarians from diverse backgrounds into the profession. In 1997, ALA established the Spectrum Scholarship to spearhead this effort. The initiative has not been overwhelmingly successful; however, it has sparked efforts to look beyond the characteristics of the workforce and concentrate on training the workforce already in place to be more responsive to issues of diversity. In that regard, the Association for College and Research Libraries promulgated a new standard in 2012 entitled Diversity Standards: Cultural Competency for Academic Libraries (ACRL Racial and Ethnic Diversity Committee 2012). The 11 standards reflect much of the discussion in this chapter and cover effects on personal growth, library collection development, services, and effects outside the library. In the rest of the chapter, we will look at three lenses that can be used to engage the questions of diversity and to bring real change to the community college environment. Multicultural and multilingual librarianship, cultural competence, and emotional intelligence are ways to challenge your assumptions about diverse clients in order to serve them better.

Multicultural and Multilingual Librarianship

The *21st Century Community College Librarian Survey* revealed that only 30 percent of community college librarians speak a second language fluently (see Appendix B). How does one reach out to users who might come to the library with any of 150 languages as their main language? The goal should not be to help everyone in their native language but to have aids in place that can help them bridge the gap of their understanding of libraries to gain the information that they are seeking. That means that librarians can use simple techniques to help a Spanish speaker understand the difference between a bookstore and the library (see My Story at the end of the chapter. In addition, the library should reflect the language and culture of the constituents in the collection and the environment. Clara Chu (2004) writes that the reason that multicultural library services should be developed is not simply for the people of diverse backgrounds who will be served but for those of the majority culture to broaden their horizons by contact with the materials and services provided.

Cultural Competence

The concept of cultural competence, also known as crosscultural competence, was developed primarily in the business world for the ever-expanding globalization of multinational corporations and others doing business abroad. It has been investigated in health care, education, and libraries because the world has come to the United States. Immigration, birth rates, and other factors have changed the U.S. population to such a degree that by the year 2050, the majority of people will be from minority communities. Cultural competence is a learned skill that must be part of every library service provider's tool kit.

The basic premise of cultural competence is that a professional must be able to understand and therefore respect another culture no matter what the source of difference might be. The stages toward gaining competence were first described by Cross et al. (1989) and have been adopted for different situations. Patricia Overall (2009) writes that the stages lie on a continuum that is linearly progressive. She places six stages of competence along one axis and shows activities that might be used to move from one stage to another. A more useful way to visualize these stages is as a circle that may be repetitious as a librarian encounters the many cultural differences that may exist in the community college (see Figure 10.1).

The goal is cultural proficiency, which is broad-based cultural competence. An individual may start at cultural blindness, where every culture will look or have the feeling that it should look like the one of our origins. Cultural incapacity may be a bit worse, because people in this stage actively seek to ignore cultural differences. A lack of cultural competence is when people are simply ignorant of differences. The stages of cultural competence may move through understanding one particular

Figure 10.1   Cultural Competence Model. Cultural competence is a learned skill that moves from cultural blindness toward cultural proficiency. At each stage various activities can help the librarian to move from one stage to the next. Cultural proficiency is reached when institutional policies and procedures have been adapted to accommodate all cultures. Although proficiency allows the culturally competent to be better at working with all cultures, individuals may find themselves moving through the circle multiple times as differences are encountered.

culture to being comfortable with multiple cultures. The stages are neither exclusive nor absolute for all cultures. A person may be culturally competent with one culture but not another.

Workshops and other training can be held to move people from cultural incapacity to more competence. Cooper, He, and Levin (2011) urge educators to push themselves beyond a comfortable cultural competence toward a critical stance toward this important set of skills. From a critical standpoint, librarians would be self-reflective about their own identities and experiences, be willing to explore and celebrate their students' cultural heritage, and transform their library services and teaching to support student success. The authors provide an overview of work by Milner (2010) that lays out five principles that should always be included in such workshops:

- *Color blindness*—As noted above, the inability to see individuals and their culture lies at the heart of cultural incompetence

- *Cultural conflict*—Librarians should be aware of the inherent power they possess as members and representatives of the dominant culture. Confronting issues of power must be part of the learning process in diversity work.

- *Myth of meritocracy*—The myth is that anyone who works hard will progress in U.S. society. The fact is that structural barriers still exist for students and faculty who do not start life in the dominant culture.

- *Deficit conceptions*—The word "impoverished" sums up this system of thinking about people. People with this view are deficient but have themselves become that characteristic. Confronting how to describe people from diverse backgrounds can transform how service is provided for their use.

- *Expectations*—Every student has something to contribute to their community. The expectation should be that each should do their best.

Cooper, He, and Levin (2011 describe a number of exercises that can be done in workshop settings to expand attendees' cultural competence. One of the most basic is to increase self-awareness by writing an autobiographical sketch that details your cultural background. The authors ask people to answer four basic questions:

1. *Explain your family origin and heritage*. Start with when your family first came to the United States, and then explain your family story.
2. *Neighborhood*. Who were your neighbors? How has your locale changed since you lived there?
3. *Schools or Libraries*. Who are the librarians that you remember? Do you remember anything that changed how you work with cultural diversity now?
4. *Cultural Self-perception vs. Cultural Perception of Others*. What cultural groups do you name as your own? Where would others classify you?

As the cultural competency continuum indicates, self-awareness is but a first step toward cultural competence. Real proficiency is at the organizational and institutional level. The library can promote cultural competence in the entire organization by promoting their diverse collections, hosting programs in the library, and being role models for their peers and students. As the Association for College and Research Libraries (ACRL) standards note, library leaders should be influential in empowering colleagues and constituents from diverse backgrounds to share their stories.

One method for achieving this is to host a diversity Book Club. Cooper et al. (2011) suggest a list of nonfiction books that can be used to stimulate conversation among library staff, faculty, students, and administrators. The powerful narratives in diverse fiction works might be even more effective in creating a space for people to tell their stories. As librarians, we can find resources that can be shared widely. In addition, librarians might host a storytelling time in which people can tell their own tales of living in a diverse world. These could be recorded and archived on a website with the proper permissions.

Using Emotional Intelligence

Emotional intelligence, also known as social and emotional learning, was described in chapter 7 as a skill for being successful with people. It is another learned skill that has been touted widely in K-12 education reform and other venues. The core competencies for SEL are self-management, self-awareness, social awareness, relationship skills, and responsible decision making. Camila Alire (2007) writes that self-awareness is the first step in being an emotionally intelligent leader in a diverse organization, just as it was for cultural competence. She writes that social awareness is the next step, and the exercises to build knowledge of other cultures can help in cultivating this skill. Finally, Alire notes that relationship management skills are essential for leadership, and it can be argued that they are important for all members of an organization. Especially important is acknowledging the role of empathy and sensitivity in influencing people's behavior. Using social emotional learning can bring an organization closer to fulfilling the ACRL standards for diversity.

International Community Colleges

The phenomenon of community colleges has spread beyond the United States (Raby and Valeau 2008; Elsner et al. 2008). Some exchange programs are being developed that mirror the study abroad programs at the university level. Supporting these programs can be important way to increase the cultural competence of the library staff and users. Build a collection that prepares students to go to overseas sites and support visitors from other countries to your institutions when they come. Try to insert yourself into the planning process for these programs. Hold the planning sessions in the library, and share the concepts of cultural competence to help students succeed in their global encounter. In addition, you might make contact with libraries in the partner institutions to see if you might hold joint programs that are hosted on a webinar service. One of the important tasks of librarianship is providing the information that people need, and these programs are another opportunity to make that happen.

RELATIONSHIP BUILDING

How do you connect with your user communities? Librarians can learn from new research that is being done in organizational communication on the power of sharing your story and having your community members share theirs. Libraries are no longer the place where books can be found; there must be other reasons for students and faculty to come to the library or the library's website.

The library's website is not just a list of links but the portal to your digital branch library. It must have what King (2009) calls real staff, real collection, real building, and real community. The website must mimic what is being done in the physical space and invite people to use both. Community members must find themselves there on the pages and in the stacks. Both must reflect the wide diversity that was outlined at the beginning of this chapter. Research by Pampaloni and Bird (forthcoming) indicates that community colleges are not yet doing a good job of creating these digital branch libraries. They did not have chat reference links, easy-to-find tutorials, and new book lists. They also did not have spaces for feedback or even clear ways of contacting the library by phone or e-mail. The point is not just one-way communication from the library to the users, but a way to build that real community.

MY STORY—BEING OPEN TO WHAT YOU DO NOT KNOW

My community college was located in a former factory building. It had long corridors and no windows. Most of the student-oriented services were on the first floor arranged side by side in a row. Many times, students would come in and ask for a textbook. I would repeat an often-told tale of not being able to afford to supply every textbook in the library. The student, often with a Latino accent, would explain that he wanted to buy the book. I would explain that you could buy the book at the bookstore down the hall. I do not know any Spanish so did not know that the word library looks more like *libreria*, the Spanish word for bookstore, than *biblioteca*, the Spanish word for library. A bit more attention to the multilingual and multicultural issues in my environment would have allowed me to help all those people much more easily. Once I knew what assumptions the students were making, I could point them in the right direction more quickly and explain that we are the *biblioteca*, come back and see us sometime.

FINAL WORDS

Diversity can be viewed through many different dimensions. This chapter looked in-depth at services for some groups of individuals in this chapter, but service is provided to one student at a time. Wherever you are on the cultural competence circle with any of the groups mentioned above, pledge to move to the next level. If you are at the "Some or limited cultural competence" stage with respect to sexual orientation, then perhaps you can host a book club on that issue that will move you and those on your staff, or even the college's staff, to cultural proficiency. Or you could work on your own cultural competence autobiography and see where improvements could be made. Everyone has moments of cultural blindness, but one can work every day to bring in new understanding.

11

INTRODUCTION TO TECHNOLOGY

In the spring of 2012, the authors taught a course in the Master of Library and Information Science (MLIS) program at the University of North Carolina at Greensboro that focused on community college libraries. During that semester, they sent an informal poll to the Association for College and Research Libraries Community (ACRL) and Junior College Section listserv asking what technologies our students should know in order to thrive in their organizations. The list that was compiled included more than 50 entries and covered a spectrum from Microsoft software applications to open-source e-learning platforms. These were far too extensive to cover in a single chapter, so major topics are chosen that highlight the most important points in each. A theme that pervades this review is the tension between do-it-yourself, or open-source solutions, and off-the-shelf, or proprietary technologies. Different libraries and consortia of libraries will choose the solution that best fits their situation.

Hopefully, what is covered will inspire students and practicing librarians to try new applications and think about how various programs and technologies can be used in the learning resources center. This overview ends with a list of organizations, websites, and conferences that can be used to keep up with the moving target that is library-related technology.

DOCUMENT PRODUCTION AND OTHER OFFICE PROCESSES

Libraries are organizations like any other business and need to produce documents, keep track of budgets, and create presentations. The most widely used set of programs is Microsoft Office, but alternatives have been proliferating. This section reviews the broad uses of Microsoft Office tools, introduces alternatives, and takes a look at storage of documents in the cloud.

Microsoft Office

Microsoft Office Suite was cited the most times as essential by the respondents to our question. Although it seems that everyone knows about all of the pieces of Microsoft Office, many new librarians don't know how to apply the capabilities of these programs to the library setting. Below is a brief introduction to each of the programs with a few examples of how they might be used.

- *Access*—This relational database program is probably the least known of all of the components. It can be useful to move collections of records into Access so that the collection can be manipulated outside of the integrated library system (ILS). For instance, it might be worthwhile to be able to have a separate database that lists all of the fiction titles that the library owns. That database could be queried by date, author, or title, and deselection decisions could be made using that. Unique databases can also be created using Access. Small collections of archival materials, equipment, or DVDs might be listed here rather than entered into the ILS. Information from Access can be exported to Excel for easier manipulation of statistics.

- *Excel*—Although mostly thought of for budgeting and other financial operations, Excel is useful for presenting statistics, keeping inventory lists, and translating data from larger systems for better control. Some libraries use Excel to create metadata that can be batch loaded into content systems like CONTENTdm. The same sort of import can be done in Access.

- *PowerPoint*—Almost everyone has done a PowerPoint slideshow in which they click through the slides, but it can also be used to present stand-alone tutorials and as a template for creating posters. Prezi is a widely used alternative that allows for nonlinear presentations. Glogster is a free way to create electronic posters that are eye-catching on large monitors and other display techniques.

- *Publisher*—Although very similar to Word, Publisher produces better pamphlets, booklets, and other small multipage documents. If you know Word, then it has a very small learning curve, but a good introduction is recommended.

- *Word*—Using Word is ubiquitous in any office setting including all libraries. It is essential to know how to create professional documents. It is a plus to know how to teach the essentials to others as many learning resource centers also teach computing basics in addition to information literacy classes.

Substitutes for using Microsoft programs are proliferating and include Open Office (OpenOffice.org), Google Docs, and LibreOffice (http://www.libreoffice .org/features/). Table 11.1 shows the features that are available in each of the alternatives recommended in recent reviews (Beal 2012; DesMarais 2011).

Cloud Computing

As noted in Table 11.1, a singular advantage of the Microsoft Office alternatives is that some of them include the option to create and then store your documents and other files on the Web rather than on a single computer's hard drive. With the proliferation of mobile devices and tablets such as the iPad, storing documents so that they are accessible from multiple devices is essential. Google Docs or Google Drive is probably the most popular version of these services. However, Dropbox is

Table 11.1 Microsoft Office Alternatives

Tool Suite	Cloud Accessible	Documents	Spread-sheets	Database	Presentations	Draw
Googledocs	✓	✓	✓	✓	✓	✓
LibreOffice		✓	✓	✓	✓	✓
Lotus Symphony		✓	✓	✓		
Open Office		✓	✓	✓	✓	✓
Zoho	✓	✓	✓	✓	✓	✓

a strong second, although it is a paid service after the first 2 GB. These services provide another great advantage by allowing easy collaboration with colleagues and are useful for sharing documents between students and professors.

AUDIO, PHOTOGRAPHS, AND VIDEO

Librarians need to create interesting presentations for instructional classes and other audiences. A basic knowledge of audio, photo, and video editing can be helpful to these endeavors. In addition, knowledge of how to share this content is important. Both are discussed in this section.

Audio can be captured digitally on many devices from your desktop computer to your smart phone. The sound quality can be enhanced by a simple microphone, but better microphones make a difference. Often it is desirable to edit these simple captures before sharing them with a podcasting service. Audacity is free and one of the most popular tools to accomplish these tasks.

A wide variety of photo-editing programs are available. For professional photographs, nothing is better than Adobe Photoshop, but the cost is prohibitive and the learning curve steep. Many other alternatives are free or bundled with other services. Microsoft Office comes bundled with a simple photo editor. Google+ has photo storage and an editing system that used to be called Picasa. The most touted alternative to Photoshop is Gnu Image Manipulation Program (GIMP), a free open-source product that can retouch photographs and convert images from one format to another.

Sharing audiovisual content sometimes requires the ability to stream from your website or the use of a streaming system such as YouTube. A private YouTube channel can be created that can hold both audio and video files. Short video and audio files can be posted in e-learning systems, inserted into instructional videos, and made available on websites for downloading.

E-LEARNING

Information literacy instruction has moved online. Librarians are embedded in classes on learning management platforms and are presenting instruction through webinars and other presentation venues. This section will look at tutorial and game production, learning management systems, and webinar presentation and live streaming.

Tutorials and Games

Many people learn from short video presentations that show them step by step how to use a particular library resource. These short videos can be used by themselves or in an instructional class to avoid using live demonstrations that rely on an Internet connection and availability of the resource you are demonstrating. Camtasia is the premier software program for producing these tutorial videos. The paid program allows for voice-over and editing and produces sharp and updateable products. The free version of Camtasia is called Jing. It can produce a video up to five minutes in length with a voice-over. It cannot be edited. That means it is best used for quick demos rather than for tutorials that will be used again and again.

Games have been shown to be great motivational tools for learning. Several free programs can be used to create your own games. These include Hot Potatoes, JeopardyLabs, and Quandary. Amy Harris Houk and Scott Rice from the University of North Carolina at Greensboro created an information literacy game (University Libraries n.d.) that can be adapted to suit your needs. These games can be played in groups or by a single player and used as a pretest of IL skills. When done in the classroom, they can be adapted to be used with clickers or real-time polling software such as Poll, everywhere that allows students to input answers via their mobile devices or classroom computers or laptops.

Results from these games can be used to provide an assessment of information literacy instruction effectiveness. Another way to assess is to use before and after online surveys. Free survey sites include SurveyMonkey, Urtak, and Zoomerang. Google Docs can be used to set up an online form that can act as a survey, as well. The results are displayed in a spreadsheet that can be downloaded and manipulated to create graphs and charts.

Learning Management Systems

The number of learning management systems (LMS) has exploded since they came on the scene in the mid-1990s. The tools in this section are sometimes referred to as course management systems or virtual learning environments. The content in these systems is related to a particular course and can be used to hold content and create class discussion boards as an adjunct to a face-to-face class, a model that is called hybrid or blended. The other model is for the entire class to be conducted online. Every college uses its LMS in different ways.

Just like ILS systems, LMS systems are either proprietary or open source. There are advantages and disadvantages to each setup. Whatever the system, librarians should know enough about it to understand how to be linked through electronic reserves in classes, to be able to embed themselves as teaching assistants or another role in the system, and to help students use the system. Working with instructional technology staff to embed a link to the library in every class and to offer stand-alone tutorials on how to find and use library systems is crucial to reaching out to distance students.

Webinar Presentation

Collaborate is the interactive webinar, meeting, or class presentation tool that is now part of Blackboard. If your school owns a Blackboard installation, then it probably has Collaborate capability. It allows a moderator to upload and give PowerPoint presentations, share a desktop, and present websites. Librarians might use the system to present classes to distance students, to create stand-alone tutorials, or to have meetings. GoToMeeting by Citrix is a commercial alternative that can be used for about $500 a year. Zoho Show, Google Hangouts, Join.me, and Skype are alternatives for small group meetings. A similar but different tool is to capture any lecture with something like Camtasia Relay by TechSmith, Tegrity Campus (by McGraw-Hill), or Panopto. Some of these systems allow live streaming or broadcasting the lecture on the web with recording available.

WEB SKILLS

The web is now the basic tool of librarianship. It connects us to our proprietary databases, allows us to search free web content, and houses our cloud-based files. Some of the web should be monitored for updates and new services. This section reviews browsers, search engines, website production, and Library 2.0 technologies.

Browsers

Nothing happens on the web without a browser program to make the connection to websites and the cloud. Each of the four major browsers has different capabilities, and they are constantly changing. Safari works primarily with Apple products. Windows Explorer is bundled with all major PC brands. Mozilla Firefox is open source and has a broad range of capabilities, including a direct connection with Zotero, the citation manager mentioned above. Google Chrome is the most recent entrant in this arena, and it seems to combine much of the others' functionality and also works with both platforms. Websites function differently depending on the browser, so it is important to have the most current version of your preferred browser. Databases, e-learning platforms, and other web-based services can behave differently when using a particular browser, so knowing more than one is essential.

Search Engines

Everyone knows Google, so is there any reason to explore other search engines? Google certainly won the war of search engines, but it is important to know that the other products do provide a different experience based on the algorithms that underlie their information retrieval and presentation in ranked lists. Bing, Yahoo, and Ask are still viable search engines, though they are used far less than Google. One recommendation is to run occasional test searches on each of these to see if you should both use and teach these alternatives.

Websites

Website design capability has many levels from very simple to very complicated. Every librarian should be able to design a simple website with basic HTML. More complicated website-building programs like Dreamweaver have a much steeper learning curve. However, simple websites can be created in Google Sites, on Wordpress, or other similar sites such as Weebly, Jimdo, or Squarespace. Although these do not have the functionality of most Dreamweaver-built websites, the programs are much easier to learn and are quite powerful. In addition, they are cloud oriented, so that a library does not have to run their own server space or take up the college's bandwidth with library traffic.

Wordpress and other services are sometimes called content management systems because they can also host blogs and other content. Open-source content management systems are becoming popular, with dotCMS being a prime example of this type of system.

LibGuide was mentioned in chapter 3 as a tool developed by Springshare Inc. to present library pathfinders and other library resource lists. Many librarians are using this platform to power their websites, as well. More and more colleges are bringing websites under a single domain that is often controlled by the information technology department. That sort of centralized control can stifle librarians' efforts to communicate with their users in a way that is responsive and interactive. By placing their main website within the LibGuide umbrella, librarians in small libraries can take back the control they need without having a web developer on staff.

A library's website is one of its most important communication tools, and one major consideration is that it be designed in accordance with accepted ADA compliance standards. The Web Accessibility Initiative website is packed with information about how to bring your website into compliance. As noted in chapter 10, librarians can lead the charge to make the campus accessible to all of the college's constituents. The website is part of that ethical responsibility.

Library 2.0

For some time, Library 2.0 has been touted as the wave of the future. In the early rush to adopt, librarians tried many of these communication avenues, but they quickly fell into disrepair from lack of monitoring. Maintaining a web presence is not a part-time activity. It must be built into a particular person's job responsibilities. Many large libraries have full-time user-experienced librarians who monitor the website, keep up the Facebook presence, and keep a Twitter account active. Those librarians report that two hours a day is spent in this way.

It may seem impossible for a small staff to do this kind of communication, but it is an essential part of being present to your community. Just as learning resource centers were located in the center of campus, you must be able to reach out with your electronic presence. The website and library 2.0 activities are simply an extension of that. These activities build ongoing relationships that can be an important part of student success.

Another way to build relationships is with the faculty you serve. Facebook, LinkedIn, Ning, and Piazza are free or low-cost ways to link small groups of people together. Private groups can be formed that are separate from the large broadcast systems like Facebook. For instance, if you connect the entire faculty who teach English 101 in one of these groups, then they and you can share assignment ideas, tips on resources, and new resources that have been received in the library.

CONTENT MANAGEMENT SYSTEMS

Librarians manage records for content, links to content, and complete content in a wide variety of computer systems. This section introduces catalogs, electronic resource management systems, and full content management systems.

Catalogs and Integrated Library Systems

The library catalog was one of the first library systems to be automated. Many of these systems were experimental and built by individual librarians for their libraries until a few commercial companies succeeded in the market. They were designed to handle the book collection after the material was already acquired. In the 1990s, their capabilities were expanded to include acquisitions and journal holdings, and they are now called integrated library systems (ILS). An order for materials of all types can be entered into the system and then tracked through receiving, cataloging, and circulation. Catalogs are the basis for circulation systems because a barcode or RFID tag is embedded in the local catalog record. RFID is used primarily in libraries that have multiple campus locations. It allows location information to be updated upon circulation of the item. Materials do not have a fixed location but can be moved from one place to another, and the catalog record will reflect that information. Electronic reserves are also usually managed through the ILS.

The ever-changing list of ILS vendors will not be duplicated here. Instead, refer to the *American Libraries* Buyers Guide, maintained by the American Library Association (ALA). Vendors who are corporate sponsors of ALA are highlighted, so it is not unbiased, but it is a comprehensive list of technology and other vendors. Most community colleges are in a consortium with other colleges or sometimes regional systems, so it is rare for a single college to make a decision about an ILS. Choosing a vendor is not a simple matter, and there are books that have been written to help those who need to engage the question (see, e.g., Webber and Peters 2010).

The primary method for obtaining catalog records is through OCLC Inc. It is the oldest shared catalog system in the United States. The company now provides a searchable catalog of their members' holdings in a web-based, free product called Worldcat. In order to add your own holdings or to edit the records, a library must be an OCLC member. That membership allows your holdings to be seen by others, which facilitates interlibrary loan on a nationwide basis. Book vendors like Yankee Book Peddler/Baker & Taylor can provide these records for the titles that a library buys, and there are companies like Marcive Inc. that will provide records for anything that you collect. In addition, Marcive and its competitors can help with retrospective conversion and other catalog-related activities, such as moving a collection from Dewey to Library of Congress classification.

Many small library collections have found that GoodReads and LibraryThing, free or low-cost personal book collection catalogs, are useful for sharing the contents of their libraries with the outside world. These services do not allow for circulation, but records can be searched on the web, and they are interactive; they allow users to express their own opinions about books and other materials. They also provide extra content like published book reviews, user reactions, and author profiles. Some community college libraries use these systems to list their new books and allow users to share book club-oriented reader reactions.

Electronic Resource Management Systems

ILS systems were designed to handle analog collections of books, journal titles, and magazine issues. The move toward electronic materials has necessitated a separate system that is used to manage passwords to all electronic subscription content, to keep track of database use licenses, and to collect statistics. Another important aspect of electronic resource management is allowing user access to the systems through IP authentication and proxy servers. They also keep track of what journals are in what database. Many of these systems are add-ons to existing ILS installations but can also be purchased separately. The systems often come loaded with information about commonly held titles.

Discovery Systems and Federated Search

In order to search all library content with a single search statement or query, a super search engine can be added to many ILS systems. These add-ons were first called federated search engines, but newer generations of them are usually called discovery systems. They require that databases that are leased by a library be open to the search engine for indexing of their content. That index is primarily on keywords from titles, subject headings, and authors. When a search is executed, the results list contains books, journals, videos, and other content. Links to full-text journal content are usually provided.

Discovery systems are being widely implemented in academic libraries (Wang and Dawes 2012) despite some of the problems that have been encountered (Kelley 2012). Some important databases have refused to be open to these systems, including the important PsycINFO database from the American Psychological Association. Users are unaware that they may be missing this vital index and its journal content in their search results. The systems work better when the databases share the same subject heading or thesaurus system. In addition, the long lists of retrieval are off-putting to some users, who have difficulty finding the most recent materials in the avalanche. The ease of use is a decided advantage; however, that will spur the further development of these systems.

Digital Libraries

Digital libraries, archives, or museums are created in systems that display digitized or born digital content on the Web. The most widely used system in U.S. libraries is CONTENTdm, a product from OCLC Inc. It uses the record structure, also called a metadata scheme, Dublin Core, which is simple and relatively straightforward. Record and object are linked together in a way that cannot happen in a standard book catalog.

Metadata intimidates the uninitiated because the word and the descriptions of it come from computer science. However, it is the essence of what librarians have always done: describe objects in a structured way so that other people can find them. That was once books and now is digital photographs, texts, and computer files. The structure can include simple fields like title, subject, and geographic location, but can also be quite complicated by describing the technical properties of the image and how it was produced.

Digitized content can be created in-house or outsourced to another entity. Lyrasis, a regional OCLC affiliate, offers a Digitization Collaborative that reduces the cost to members. North Carolina has a state-funded collaboration run by the University of North Carolina at Chapel Hill. In-house digitization works for small projects, but it does not scale up without investment in proper equipment, expert staff, and good facilities, usually out of reach for a single community college.

Institutional Repositories

Institutional repositories for community colleges were introduced in chapter 9. Most small colleges will want to join a consortium of schools that will organize and display the intellectual output of their faculty. Several ILS vendors have developed add-ons that can be used as institutional repositories; for instance, Innovative Interfaces has a system for digital asset management called ContentPro that could be used as a repository.

Open-Source Systems

The alternative to proprietary systems is to use an open-source system such as Koha, Drupal, DSpace, or Greenstone as content management systems. The major disadvantage is the expertise needed to manage such a system. Knowledge of network and server management is needed to manage the installation and configuration of these systems. The learning curve is not impossible, but it requires more expertise than a librarian in a single institution can usually apply to the problem. Some large systems have done this, however; for instance, the State of Georgia created and manages the Evergreen system that all Georgia libraries use.

PERSONALIZED INFORMATION ORGANIZATION AND MANAGEMENT

Librarians need to keep track of their own information sources, and they should know how to teach others to manage theirs. Current awareness of new information and managing what you have already found are the hallmarks of librarianship.

Current Awareness Tools

Until recently, RSS feeds were one method to bring new information to your desktop from newspapers, blogs, updated website content, and journals. Mobile apps are the latest innovation for connecting to and monitoring constantly updating content. In turn, managing apps is another responsibility for librarians to embrace in helping people control their information. However, to date no good app manager has been created; most are displayed by category and product. Although seemingly useful, it is difficult to know which apps are truly useful. Reading reviews in the sources listed at the end of the chapter can help.

Citation Managers

In addition to keeping informed of new information, librarians and their users must keep track of what they have read in order to cite their sources properly. It is easy to write citations with new versions of Microsoft Word, but more sophisticated tools such as Endnote (a product from ISI), Refworks (offered by Proquest), and Zotero (free and open source), actually create a database of the materials that you have read. New articles can be added from database or web searches, either in full text or just the citation information. Articles can be stored in them and then found through searching your own database. In-text citations can be added and bibliographies constructed in almost any citation format, from that used by the American Psychological Association to the Modern Language Association's structure.

Other information managers that are useful are the social bookmarking and bibliography tools offered by sites like De.li.cious, Diigo, digg, and stumbleupon. Worldcat, LibraryThing, and GoodReads can also be used to share important websites. One caveat is that some networks bar the use of social media sites, and these are based on the same technologies. Check with your information technology department if you have trouble using these sites.

Note-Taking and More

Microsoft OneNote was one of the first products to allow full-text searching access to anything typed into the file. It is a wonderful way to cut and paste material from the web and to take notes at conferences and other meetings. Evernote is a cloud-computing solution to take notes and much more, and there are ways to use this product to keep track of photos, citations, and results from searches in databases (Miller 2010). Connecting to this product from multiple computers and mobile devices, you can keep track of all of the content you create during a day.

One other type of tool is a social media curation site, such as Storify. Media curation is the art of making sense of the immense amount of content created in blogs and social media about a particular topic. Storify and other products, like Pinterest, allow you to pull pieces of information from all over the web and make sense of it for your readers. Who better to do that for their users than librarians? More than 40 different competing products can be used for this purpose; choose one that you can adopt easily.

STAFFING FOR TECHNOLOGY

Master's-level graduates should have a thorough grounding in the use of a wide range of technologies, most of which are discussed in this chapter. The authors' survey respondents noted two areas of expertise that are not covered here, namely, network management and print management. It is true that learning resource center directors are sometimes in charge of the information technology for the entire campus, but staffing for these technical areas should be focused on information *technology* and not information organization or use. Information technology requires different training that can be at the bachelor's level or below. Staffing with paraprofessionals for these jobs is one solution to these issues. Another is to encourage MLIS staff to attend classes in computer science or network engineering programs taught at the institution in which they work. Another solution is to cultivate a work study in one of these fields who understands the needs of libraries and systems administration and hire that person when he or she graduates.

MY STORY—THE ACCIDENTAL SYSTEMS LIBRARIAN

My community college was part of a mixed-library consortium that included public libraries, small colleges, and some school libraries in our local region of Connecticut. We could tell what the local library had but not what the other community colleges owned. When the desire to share our catalogs on the web could not be met by our local consortium, we banded together with other community colleges to manage our own ILS. This required that we have an in-house systems librarian. I was the only one who raised her hand. I learned some of the intricacies of database conversion, installation of the automated check-in, and acquisitions. It was a learning curve for which I was unprepared after 10 years in the profession. Yet it was fun and interesting, and I am glad I did it. You never know what you might have to do as a community college librarian.

FINAL WORDS

Technologies are converging. Integrated library systems are now content management systems that can host digital collections or institutional repositories. Website hosting sites, like dotCMS, also host blogs, Twitter feeds, and other areas mentioned in separate sections throughout the course of this chapter. Mobile apps are proliferating for every conceivable library service. Keeping your skills up-to-date requires effort, but there are many places that you can find help.

The major source of help is ALA and its many divisions and subdivisions. Those that are related to technology are:

- Library and Information Technology Association (LITA). They publish *Information Technology and Libraries* and a list called Top Tech Trends http://www.ala.org/lita/professional/trends

- Association for Library Collections and Technical Services (ALCTS). *Library Resources & Technical Service* (http://www.ala.org/alcts/resources/lrts) is the journal that they produce. In addition, they hold many webinars on dealing with ILS and other automated systems.

- Association for College and Research Libraries (ACRL). This division publishes its own take on technology in http://acrl.ala.org/techconnect/.

ALA's journal, *American Libraries*, has many articles about technology issues. Already mentioned above is the Buyers Guide that they publish at http://americanlibrariesbuyersguide.com/. ALA also presents the website ALA techsource. That website also includes a link to *Library Technology Reports* that are available for about $50 per issue or through some databases.

Other organizations that relate to information technology can also be useful to librarians. The American Society for Information Science and Technology publishes research on these topics in their publication *JASIST*. Educause (http://www.educause.edu/) is an organization that works at the college level; in other words, institutions are members of Educause, and information technology departments are usually the representatives appointed to attend meetings. Their publications can be useful, especially *Educause Review*. The Association for Educational Communication and Technology (AECT) represents the other IT, instructional technology. The ongoing relationship between AECT and K-12 library standards has not yet been made explicit to academic libraries. Nonetheless, their publications and conferences can be helpful to some library applications, especially in the area of distance and online learning.

Webinars are offered on an occasional basis by these organizations, but there are less expensive sources. Webjunction, at http://www.webjunction.org, serves as a clearinghouse of training sessions that are both online and face-to-face. Major technology vendors will also offer training, sometimes at your institution when there is enough interest.

Every ALA and state library association conference has vendor exhibits that can inform you about technology. An annual conference called Computers in Libraries is sponsored by Information Today, a leading publisher of books about this topic. It is one conference that includes presentations by librarians and information/ instructional technology personnel, thereby giving a broad perspective on the issues.

Major journals that are worth following are *Computers in Libraries*, *Library Technology Reports*, *American Libraries*, especially the columns called the "Internet Librarian" and "Technology in Practice"; and *Library Journal*, including the "Digital Libraries" column. Some information technology publications, like *PC World* or *MacWorld*, can be helpful but do not have the library focus in mind. Reasonably unbiased hardware and software reviews are also available from CNET.com. For help with instruction, it is also worth following the ProfHacker column from *The Chronicle of Higher Education*.

Some columnists have their own blogs on the publication websites that are worth following, notably Roy Tennant, Marshall Breeding, and Joseph Janes. Many of these same influential writers are active on Twitter. Other library gurus that you should follow on Twitter or through their blogs are Michael Stephens, Amanda Goodman, and Troy Swanson, a fellow community college librarian.

12

ASSESSMENT

Assessment has become an important and growing area of community college libraries' functionality and can provide the data and evidence needed to make decisions related to resource allocation, effect of library services in the larger institution, and advocacy for needed support to achieve mission goals. Because resources are tight, it is important for community colleges to determine what materials, services, and investments are important and which ones are not in order to focus attention on areas that will provide the best return on investment. This includes use of space, measuring student learning outcomes from instruction, purchases of resources, competencies of staff fulfilling specific services, and other areas of involvement or expectations of the libraries within the community college arena.

Assessment is vital because community colleges play a vital role in workforce development and preparing students for more advanced educational opportunities. Measurements of the effectiveness of services to students and faculty can be used to meet accreditation guidelines for continued survival and support. It can show how the library participates in reaching the learning goals that are achieved on campus. By developing and sustaining an assessment program to cover a wide variety of areas, librarians can effectively make changes or pursue courses of action that have a greater effect while at the same time providing the opportunity to advocate for the resources needed to make those changes or pursue those service needs.

In defining the purpose for conducting assessment activities of any given area, the overall role of the library on campus should be considered so that assessment efforts can be focused accordingly. For example, the library can be considered to be many things to different campus groups. The library brings together people with various information needs to use resources and guidance, both physically and virtually. That simple sentence can become very complicated in practice, as the librarian must consider multiple derivations of people's needs, resources and formats; physical space and use; virtual and remote needs and expectations; not to mention ongoing and constant changes to any or all of those elements.

Other nontangible roles that the library might play include how the library facilitates knowledge or knowledge transfer. This would include such things as how the environment is created to foster learning activities, or how staff engages patrons and offers guidance or structure to the use of resources, and how information literacy is taught and embraced as a developing skill for lifelong use. All of these opportunities provide ample reasons for conducting assessment in order to measure and evaluate current situations so that future actions and activities are improved and more efficient.

PURPOSEFUL ASSESSMENT

Purposeful assessment indicates that the library as an organization is interested in growth and improvement of services, facilities, staffing, resources, and any other activity that is subject to consideration by stakeholders for continuance or removal. It is recommended that this be done proactively instead of being imposed from the outside or forced to correct a problem. The three general areas to consider when developing a program are:

- *Purpose*—what is meant to be evaluated for improvement
- *Methodology*—what is the best method or methods for assessing this particular purpose and reporting strategy
- *Results*—what is the best way to use the results or data obtained

The basic elements begin with a statement of purpose or problem statement. This should provide the context in which the assessment will occur and address the concerns or reasons for the evaluation. Most problem statements should represent the stakeholder point of view and include the focus and scope of what and how much are being assessed. Background information is given and, if applicable, a historic context from which the situation has developed. This is where limitations should be addressed or included that could affect the problem. Limitations should not be defensive but open and transparent so as to get a true understanding as you move forward.

At this point, a literature review is helpful, especially when multiple issues are being addressed, so that relevant or similar activities can be vetted for guidance or best practices. The last 5 to 10 years have seen an increase in professional development activities related to assessment, and the literature has many examples to pull from and learn or tweak to fit a customized need. It is also important to gather secondary or supporting data that can be applied to the situation to support the objectives or problem to be assessed. For example, when studying building use, having circulation stats or gate counts for the entrances provides some context for assessing other attributes.

Next, it is important to determine assessment objectives, which in turn will help narrow down the research questions to ask. For example, a problem statement regarding a building renovation might have as an objective to determine user furniture needs for studying or group activities; or a reason to conduct an assessment of library instruction might have as an objective to determine if students learned to evaluate resources properly. Open-ended assessment is problematic because it can lose focus if information is collected too broadly.

DATA TYPES AND METHODOLOGIES

As mentioned earlier, secondary and support data will help define the assessment need and focus on new data to be learned. An assessment program is like a research project, and gathering data is the foundation from which results will be written and acted upon. It is important to consolidate all relevant data from many sources. Data types include:

Primary data, which is gathered firsthand and includes data gathered from assessments:

- Experiments or testing
- Surveys
- Interviews
- Focus groups
- Direct observation

Secondary or supporting data, which is usually gathered by others or as a result of documenting processes:

- Secondhand or generated reports
- Historical data
- Purchased data
- Professional publications
- Benchmarking with similar institutions
- Best-practices comparisons

The common methods for obtaining primary data for assessment purposes include surveys or questionnaires, interviews, focus groups, and observation. Each has advantages and disadvantages and should be carefully considered in determining the assessment strategy. The method chosen should be reflective of the context in which the problem exists and the format in which data is needed.

Surveys or questionnaires are one of the most popular methods used for assessments in libraries because they are the most cost effective for gathering a large quantity of feedback. ARL's LibQUAL uses this method, and this allows ARL to create a large database of benchmarking data for participating schools to compare themselves against. Another advantage is that the data is usually collected anonymously with perhaps some demographic components but not at individual identifiers. They are also quick and easy to do simultaneously and in multiple locations. This also can create disadvantages based on the research need, since surveys are impersonal and can lack the detail or explanation needed from a deeper or wider point of view, such as with a focus group or individual interview.

Another popular method of assessment is to conduct focus groups with stakeholders who understand the information you want to know. Focus groups can gain more data than individual interviews because you include multiple people at once and you also benefit from the group interaction because this might draw out points of view not considered previously. An important component of focus groups are the nonverbal clues that an experienced facilitator can use to "dig deeper" for certain types of information or perspectives on the subject. Focus groups can be a teaching tool as well by sharing information or secondary data with the group; comments and answers can be learned and kept realistic or useful in terms of creating solutions from the data obtained.

Individual interviews provide a more personal experience and allow the researcher to obtain more details and explore the problem or issue with more clarity. Although questions should still be structured, the free association allows for follow-ups and clarification questions that can provide insights not gained from mass responses to a single point of query and allows for anecdotes, stories, and descriptive examples to put the data gained into the correct context. The interview method takes more time, which can be more costly, as well as reducing the size of the interview sample, if that is a factor. It also is important for an experienced, nonbiased interviewer who is skilled at exploring all options to conduct the sessions. Interviewees should also be chosen in such a way as to encourage a broad spectrum of ideas and viewpoints.

Observational studies are a less-used form of assessment in libraries but have strong credibility in business environments. A lot of marketing research is conducted through observational studies; one of the best-known examples comes from Paco Underhill, who wrote the bestseller *Why We Buy: The Science of Shopping*. Observational studies eliminate emotion from data because you typically are observing behaviors in which participants are unaware of being observed and act or behave naturally. Underhill's company focuses on the use of observation to record people's natural or instinctive reactions to products or environments, plus providing companies with data to influence product design, placement, and overall appeal to customers.

In a community college environment, observational studies might be useful to influence how limited resources are being used and could be focused more effectively. Observations should be structured with a checklist of observable behaviors and conducted across a variety of circumstances with persons trained on effective observation. Observing how people use your library, interact with each other and the staff, and learn in the process can be significant in making the library a source of influence and esteem.

One other seldom-used technique is *sandboxing*. This involves testing concepts or services before full implementation in order to judge value and use prior to making a larger commitment. This can also be combined with a task force that is charged with investigating a particular phenomenon and utilizes a sandbox assessment to help plot a course of action.

Some library organizations have used charettes, in particular with space assessment, to allow stakeholders to have both a say and an investment in the creation of a design or mapping activity. This method will provide overlapping segments of data but will also highlight popular choices or different perspectives than those originally thought of. Either way, it helps draw stakeholders into the process and conversation.

Finally, with regard to assessment methods, never discount the possibility of engaging experts instead of doing something on your own. This is usually more expensive, but depending on the situation and purpose, an expert in that field with credentials and qualifications specific to the research need might make a difference in how the results are viewed and provide additional support when advocating for resources. Sometimes in community college environments, outside expertise can help support issues that are more community-based for a broader spectrum of stakeholders.

USING YOUR RESULTS

The purpose that guided the assessment will lead to formulating the results for use. The publication of results should be given the same thoughtful consideration as developing the methodology and problem statements. Assessments are meant to provide facts or data that are unbiased and offers an objective approach to the situation or issue. Your results should be presented without prejudice or emotion, and this allows you to remove politics from the situation. Sometimes this is called evidence-based decision making, where decisions are made on assessment data citing the evidence provided and not the desires of those involved.

Good assessment data will also help dispel potentially adversarial situations in which conflict might be possible from opposing points of view. It takes problems out of a personal context and shows a perspective that is supported by the evidence gained from the assessment. The quality of your results becomes a consideration in implementing and executing the process, such as:

- What are the overall goals and objectives that you are collecting data for?

- What questions are you asking, and are they the right questions to get the information you need?

- Who is your audience, and should that be determined broadly or narrowly?

- What secondary sources of information are available for you to utilize in conjunction with an assessment project?

- How much monies are available to invest in an assessment project? This might be a factor in determining scope and substance.

- Is your assessment project designed to be efficient, which could influence the quality based on participants' time and effort?

Historically, results were quantitative for purposes of accreditation, certification, or as a measure of standards imposed by library associations as a means of distinction. Quantitative measures have become obsolete as institutional missions have changed and called for assessment activities to have a different point of view. In today's environment, results need to reflect our user's opinion of service quality. Community college libraries should be following standards by which individual institutions can evaluate their own performance in relation to the needs of their students and faculty as well as other user populations.

Successful assessment programs will not be one-shot activities but interpret user feedback systematically over time and develop an institution's own benchmarks for measuring success. Continuous assessment also helps an organization identify best practices across similar institutions and provides a culture of change for organizational development to ensure constant improvements over time.

LibQUAL+ AND MORE

As mentioned earlier, LibQUAL+ is a survey instrument developed by the Association of Research Libraries to aid the library community in solicitation, tracking, understanding, and acting upon how users perceive the quality of service they receive. Due to cost, many community college libraries take the survey as a group or within a consortium. The program's centerpiece is a rigorously tested, web-based survey bundled with training that helps libraries assess and improve library services, change organizational culture, and market the library. The goals of LibQUAL+ are to:

- Foster a culture of excellence in providing library service

- Help libraries better understand user perceptions of library service quality

- Collect and interpret library user feedback systematically over time
- Provide libraries with comparable assessment information from peer institutions
- Identify best practices in library service
- Enhance library staff members' analytical skills for interpreting and acting on data

A big advantage of participating in LibQUAL+ is the amount of data that has been collected, which provides benchmarking data for analyzing results. More than 1,000 libraries have participated, including a large number of community college libraries, and the instrument has been refined over time to be more compact and effective.

Other forms of assessment that are emerging include looking closer at the human side of library services and assessing the characteristics and traits found in different aspects of how students learn and go about their academic activities. Ethnography, as a subset of anthropology, looks at and describes particular cultures that we choose to be identified with. This allows for assessment of human traits such as study habits, evaluation and use of resources, or logistical characteristics of academic work in order to develop deeper results to services offered, facilities presented, and operational activities. The landmark work in this area, Foster and Gibbons's *Studying Students: The Undergraduate Research Project at the University of Rochester*, was published in 2007. This type of work is an example of how the use of ethnography methods of assessment can demonstrate a greater connection of library services and resources to the students and other users.

MY STORY

I am a former retail store manager who has embraced the use of observation as a method to influence decisions made within library environments. For example, in conducting a space assessment study, we made observational studies of students working with materials in the reference department. We observed a very low percentage of students working with library materials; they primarily worked with materials brought from outside the library. This combined with other secondary pieces of related data led us to conclude that in this situation, students who needed study space did not necessarily need access to print materials. In turn, this finding influenced decisions related to reducing the size of the print collection in favor of creating additional spaces for students to study.

FINAL WORDS

At the 2011 ACRL Conference in Philadelphia, James G. Neal of Columbia University presented his paper "Stop the Madness: The Insanity of ROI and the Need for New Qualitative Measures of Academic Library Success." In it he advocates moving away from quantitative measures like watching the numbers, number of volumes, gate counts, information session participants, etc., and focusing instead on the user and the user's needs. This was a reaction to a growing trend of assessment data aimed at justifying expense during a time of budgetary constraint. He was reminding us to follow what is important to our missions.

Assessment takes time and effort and sometimes expense, depending on method and scope; but assessment is important for evaluating what the library does within the larger institutional mission and maintaining or increasing needed resources to sustainability. Community colleges in particular are pressed to make tough economic decisions, so a library that can demonstrate its effect on students, student learning, and faculty support will endure.

13

——◦•◦——

IF YOU SUPERVISE

Chapter 7 features a discussion of leadership as it relates to individuals becoming leaders. Leaders are not always managers or supervisors but have influence over people just the same by virtue of their personality or style of developing relationships with people. Leading people is different than supervising or managing them, but sometimes you are called upon to do both. This last chapter is meant for those who might be supervising others or have more than just an informal leadership relationship. This is about basic supervisory skills and how strategic planning is important for a sustainable future for your library.

Most organizations distinguish between supervisors and leaders by addressing supervisors as frontline people who carry out short-term goals and immediate tasks assigned to individuals or groups and managers who are involved in long-term strategic planning. In a community college library, the size of the organization makes a difference; smaller units might have only one person who performs both roles, and larger and multiunit libraries might have a larger group of supervisors with a couple of administrators who help to form those strategic connections with the larger institution or community. Typical expectations of supervisors might include:

- Clarifying roles or work assignments of others:
  - assigning tasks,
  - explaining job responsibilities,
  - and setting performance expectations;
- Monitoring service provision:
  - checking on the progress,
  - troubleshooting problems,
  - and observing the quality of the work;
- Coaching and evaluating individual and unit performance;

- Short-term planning or determining how to use personnel and other resources:
  - scheduling desk times,
  - assigning reshelving responsibilities;
- Consulting or checking with people before making decisions that affect them:
  - encouraging participation in decision making,
  - using the ideas and suggestions of others;
- Supporting or being considerate:
  - showing empathy and support when someone is upset or anxious,
  - providing encouragement and support when a task is difficult or stressful;
- Recognizing and praising effective performance, significant achievements, special contributions, and performance improvements;
- Developing personnel:
  - providing opportunities for skill development,
  - helping people learn how to improve their skills;
- Empowering or allowing substantial responsibility and discretion in work activities; in other words, trusting people to solve problems and make decisions without getting approval first;
- Encouraging innovation by challenging people to question their assumptions, think about the work, and consider better ways of doing it.

Overall, the purpose of the supervisor is to work with other people in order to maximize their performance for great effectiveness by the individual and for greater efficiency for the organization. What is a leader, then? A leader is someone who reports to the outside authority and sets strategic goals for the entire organization.

SKILL SETS

Supervisors typically have strong skill sets in three general areas: technical skills, intellectual skills, and interpersonal skills. Technical skills are those related to the work being performed; intellectual skills relate to higher-level thinking; and interpersonal skills are for interacting and building relationships with others. The mix of these skill sets might be related to specific expectations for the supervisor in terms of working knowledge expected of them individually. For example, a supervisor for a technical services area might have a greater need for technical skills than someone supervising public services, while the public service manager might require more interpersonal skills. This, of course, is customized to the organization, but it is worth recognizing these differences when distributing responsibilities to individuals or making hiring decisions.

Technical skills involve having knowledge of related technical areas along with some of the history or background in the technology being used. This enables a supervisor to help problem-solve and troubleshoot issues that occur as well as train new hires or others on the processes involved. To look at the technical services area again, a supervisor in that area may need to have in-depth experience with OCLC or some other integrated library system.

Intellectual skills are important for supervisors because this is what distinguishes them from others in order to lead the organization to fulfill its mission or produce results. These skills include:

- *Planning*—building the infrastructure needed to perform tasks or gather resources
- *Organizing*—systematizing tasks and persons to complete those tasks
- *Controlling*—monitoring the progress of actions taking place in order to make changes
- *Problem solving and decision making*—addressing issues that take place in the course of doing work or providing services
- *Negotiation*—advocating for resources needed and compromising as needed
- *Time management*—keeping things on schedule and giving timely responses to stakeholders

Interpersonal skills are used with other people directly and affect how the organization functions and achieves its goals. These skills are important for both supervisors and managers to enable them to get the important work of the organization moving forward as effectively and efficiently as possible. These skills include:

- *Communication*—providing or exchanging information that is sometimes crucial for people to complete their work
- *Delegation*—sharing or distributing work to others, along with the needed information or training to perform tasks
- *Negotiation*—exchanging different points of view in order to reach a satisfactory conclusion by all involved
- *Motivation*—providing encouragement and the desire to achieve particular results by all who are performing tasks or services
- *Team building*—finding common elements of work or goals to be achieved in order to have people working together for the greater good
- *Rewarding*—recognizing the work and value of others in order to positively reinforce the worth of their efforts

All of these skills are important for the making of a good supervisor. A lot of supervisory skills are learned on the job or when someone is thrust into a situation, and thus are not always executed evenly.

Traditionally, library schools have not focused much attention on developing supervisory, management, or leadership skills. Library supervisors are usually staff members who have served the longest or seek to increase their authority over time. Thus, training for supervisory skills can be inconsistent or nonexistent. Many educational systems, library systems, professional associations, and peer-driven groups have begun to invest in providing training in the acquisition of good people skills that can translate into supervising others.

Self-training is also an option, and Samuel Certo's *Supervision: Concepts and Skill-Building* is an excellent primer for learning how to supervise others (2013). Certo identifies a positive attitude as one of the characteristics of a successful supervisor.

Employees tend to reflect the attitudes of people in charge, and this should be an all-inclusive approach to supervising others. He lists other successful traits as well:

- Successful supervisors are loyal. As a part of the management team, they must take actions that are best for the organization.

- Successful supervisors are fair, because supervisors who play favorites or behave inconsistently will lose the support and respect of their employees and not be able to perform effectively.

- Supervisors also need to be good communicators to ensure consistent execution throughout their area of responsibility.

- Supervisors must be able to delegate, that is, give their employees authority and responsibility to carry out activities.

- Successful supervisors must also want the job and not feel burdened by being responsible for the actions of others.

No matter how supervisory skills are studied and improved, doing something is far better than doing nothing if placed in a situation of supervising others. Taking advantage of learning opportunities and reflecting on growth can help a new supervisor build capacity in managing employees.

SELECTED CONCERNS

A couple of concerns to share about supervising in a community college library environment, confrontation and generational issues, warrant a little extra attention. Because of the diverse nature of community college libraries, confrontations will arise that will require mediation or an experienced point of view to resolve. Within the workplace, community college librarians can see a wide range in the ages and perceptions of staff members, which can cause problems or concerns to those supervising.

The first consideration of how a supervisor deals with confrontation is supported by a study conducted recently by Cooper and Sigmar (2012). They addressed how employees perceive constructive or corrective confrontation from supervisors and by what means it can be done beneficially. The question is particularly important in a library due to the nature of the usually congenial staff relationships that are found there. They summarize that supervisors should have training and skill development on confrontational issues that can ultimately affect organizational culture overall. Their findings also point out some other important factors.

Employees value feedback not just when it is about having done something incorrectly or needing a corrective conversation. Positive and supportive feedback can be more effective than any kind of negative feedback that resulted in the confrontation. The authors of the study also conclude that empathy and respect are valued by employees as well as supervisors having a participatory management style. This type of feedback supported employees' feelings that they were treated fairly and that there was equitable treatment of all employees. Cooper and Sigmar (2012) conclude that listening skills were identified as being important for supervisors, especially in dealing with confrontation. Sidebar 13.1 is a list of suggested resources for improving listening skills and other areas of supervision.

Sidebar 13.1 SUGGESTED RESOURCES

Free Management Library - How to Improve Your Listening Skills
http://managementhelp.org/communicationsskills/listening-skills.htm

Student Readiness Inventory Tool Shop
http://www.act.org/engage/studentguide/pdf/ImproveListening.pdf

---

Another concern to draw attention to are generational issues within the workplace. As mentioned earlier, community colleges and potentially the library as well will be made up of a wide range of age groups from staff and student workers. This can change the methods employed by supervisors to be effective and should be considered as needed. Some good examples come from the 2010 Visual Resources Association (VRA) Conference and in particular a paper submitted by Jen Green at Plymouth State University entitled "Millennials at Work: Re-imagining Communication in Order to Improve Training" (2010). Green worked with student workers on different ways of communicating, particularly with Facebook, and concluded that by keeping an open mind and encouraging the students to be involved in the process, new formats and processes for communicating with different age groups are possible. Similar work can be found in Meister and Willyerd's article on mentoring the millennial generation (2010).

The point here for anyone supervising is to recognize the value that different generational groups bring to the table and learn how to communicate and share their strengths with others in the organization. Many organizations set up seminars and presentations on working effectively between generational differences; the first step is to recognize that these groups all have different perspectives, experiences, and expectations of how to be treated. The same principles of supervision in Certo's book (2013) apply across generations, but the methods and techniques to get there can be different.

LEADERSHIP

So when does supervising become leadership? Distinct differences are identified between supervising or managing people within an organization and providing leadership. Leadership is about providing vision, goals, and objectives, and advocating for the organization at a higher level. Supervising is about implementing those visions and goals and utilizing the skills mentioned earlier for effectively moving the organization forward.

In a community college library, leaders can be anyone who has a positive influence over others and is focused on moving the library in sync with the larger organization. This can be accomplished with the relationships established throughout campus or with faculty users of the library. A small library can have multiple leaders as long as everyone is working toward a common cause.

Formally, leadership is also going to have the responsibility that comes with a formal position, like a dean or director, and the expectation of specific performance issues for the person and the library as an organization. Supervisors and managers are duty-bound to follow the formal leader's authority but can look for ways to provide constructive feedback up the organization and not just to subordinates. Abraham Zaleznik, in his classic *Harvard Business Review* article on managers and leaders, discusses the status of the leader and how they grow. He writes that leaders must also increase their ability to deal with higher-level confrontation and to cultivate the credibility needed to sustain a vision in the face of conflict (2004).

This can be important in a community college library setting because the leader of the organization must be able to advocate for needed resources but also negotiate and distribute those resources fairly across the organization. As they climb the career path toward leadership, they must develop the skills that could potentially affect any challenge to their authority as leader and visionary. Part of this process could come from how, as a leader, they approach strategic planning.

STRATEGIC PLANNING

Leaders should have a strategy. This means that a leader should have a plan of action for daily activities that affect the larger vision or mission of what is expected of the organization. Leaders should be analyzing their current situation as it relates to what they ultimately want to achieve for the larger organization. This affects supervision because it drives the work to be performed and how effectively and efficiently that occurs. An organization's overall success is directly related to the strategies that leaders employ along with how well supervisors manage the process. A community college library is no exception to this and could be a defining element in the push for resources and attention from campus administration.

Good leaders will involve their team in all aspects of developing a strategic plan. This starts with analyzing your current status or situation and how you fit into the larger plans for the college. Understanding your position within the campus and the scope of the expectations for the library in the academic environment is a great way to give your team the opportunity to see the big-picture effect that the library has on the college. Understanding the priorities of the community college as a whole can be the strongest basis for setting the library's plan for activities, services, and resource allocation.

The next step is to identify resources and emerging trends in order to determine priorities and make changes needed to direct resources and attention to areas that matter the most. This is the stage in strategic planning that could create the most conflict, including generational differences over traditional practices and methods. This is why a focus on trends or an environmental scan of the field will help provide needed information to make proper determinations. It also sets the stage for continuous review of ongoing planning and adjustments. Taking information from the assessment activities discussed in chapter 12 can help guide the setting of the strategic plan.

Eleonora Dubicki's *Strategic Planning in College Libraries*, published for ACRL, offers 25 examples of strategic plans across the country (2011). This resource can provide good ideas for addressing future library needs in a changing world.

MY STORY

I earned my library degree after a 22-year career as a retail manager. The significance of that is in the management and leadership experience. All of my library jobs have focused on my supervisory and leadership experiences and skills gained during this retail career. While I have transitioned successfully, I have observed the struggle of others who have not had this experience. Libraries, especially community college libraries, need individuals who are going to properly supervise others in order to drive the work and services that are needed, as well as leaders who will plan strategically while advocating for the library with the college. This doesn't just happen. Supervisory skills and leadership ideals should be purposefully pursued and appropriately developed for long-term leadership growth and for the sustainability of the organization, not to mention the field of librarianship.

FINAL WORDS

Many people become supervisors out of happenstance: they are senior, have superior technical skills, or talk when no one else will. A strong organization grows supervisors through thoughtful leadership and purposeful planning so that a strategy can be developed and executed that will promote the library and ensure its relevance on campus. Community colleges are making a significant contribution to America's higher education, and the community college library will need good leaders to ensure that the library is part of that experience.

Appendix A

IMLS GRANT PROPOSAL FROM 2010

University of North Carolina at Greensboro: ECCL (Educating Community College Librarians)
   Project Title: ECCL (Educating Community College Librarians): Strengthening Community College Librarianship

STATEMENT OF INTENT

The University of North Carolina at Greensboro (UNCG) Department of Library and Information Studies (DLIS) is proposing a grant-funded project to further IMLS Laura Bush 21st Century Librarian Program Priority 6, Continuing Education, in the area of community college librarianship.[1] The University was recently given a Community Engagement Classification by the Carnegie Foundation. A university-based MLIS program and community college libraries across the Southeast will work together to develop this initiative. The goal of *ECCL (Educating Community College Librarians): Strengthening Community College Librarianship* is to build a nationally recognized continuing education and MLIS curriculum that enhances the careers of practicing librarians and trains MLIS students that are ready to embark upon challenging careers in these unique institutions. The objectives to achieve these goals are:

1. **Develop a series of continuing education modules specifically for 21st century community college librarians, based on research, and situated within the MLIS program.**

   Using a participatory and collaborative approach to curriculum development called DACUM (Developing A CUrriculuM), ECCL will create continuing education modules that answer the unique and acute needs of the

---

[1]In this document librarianship, librarians, and libraries will be used to describe both libraries and learning resource centers.

community college library. Continuing education modules will be designed to help current community college librarians cope with the changing nature of their professional duties.

2. **Employing a Teaching-Librarian-Faculty practicum in participating community colleges to prepare new MLIS graduates and to enhance the careers of practicing librarians.**
   The teaching-librarian-faculty model for practicum has been piloted as a joint project between the UNCG University Libraries and the Department of Library and Information Studies. For this project, the model will be used to develop the supervisory skills of the practicing librarians, while giving the students in-depth, experiential learning opportunities within a paid practicum experience.

3. **Curriculum for MLIS students.**
   The continuing education modules will be developed in online courseware that can be combined and enhanced to serve as the basis for full-course development to be incorporated into the MLIS curriculum and offered nationally through the WISE consortium.

4. **Textbook that trains future CC librarians and helps practicing CC librarians to update their skills.** A textbook built from materials in the continuing education modules and the curriculum will be created to provide sustainability for the project.

ASSESSMENT OF NEED AND INTENDED RESULTS

Background

Recently, there has been a renewed focus on the importance of community colleges in providing post-secondary education in the United States, such as President Obama's White House Community College Summit and the accompanying statement about *Building American Skills by Strengthening Community Colleges.* Enrollments are up nationwide, as well, with a PEW Research Center analysis of 2008 enrollment trends noting that an "all-time" high college enrollment nearing 40 percent of the U.S. population was due in large part to growth in community college attendance (PEW 2008). With an illustrious history dating back to 1901, the number of community colleges in the United States has increased 17 percent between 1974 and 2006 to 1,045 in 2006–2007 (U.S. Department of Education 2008), although it may be as high as 1,078 according to a search done in the Carnegie classifications database. The number of library facilities is probably larger than that because many institutions have multiple campuses and therefore multiple libraries. In North Carolina alone, there are 59 community colleges, and many of these have more than one library facility. Central Piedmont Community College, the largest North Carolina institution, with 30,000 students, has 7 libraries.

Learner Diversity

Community colleges are different than four-year institutions. In order to understand how this might impact the librarians that serve them, personnel on the *ECCL* have been working together for the past year on a project entitled *Defining the*

Community College Librarian (DTCCL). The project launched a survey that examined a broad range of issues in community college librarianship, including workforce, resource, and governance issues. The approximate student enrollment in these colleges is over 6.2 million nationally. The colleges cater to underserved populations. For instance, in fall 2005, 19 percent of community colleges had enrollments where the percentage of minority students was the largest segment of their total enrollment. In public four-year institutions, minority student enrollment is only 15 percent and in private not-for-profit four-year institutions, that group represents only 10 percent (Provasnik and Planty 2008). In North Carolina in the 2008–2009 statistics, schools reported that 25 percent of students identified themselves as Black, 3.8 percent were Hispanic, and 4 percent were multiple or mixed races. The age range is also quite broad with only 51 percent of the students in the 18–24 year old group with a range of ages from 16 to 70. Nationally, 64 percent of students fit other parameters of the definition of nontraditional, meaning that they are financially independent, working, single parents, or with dependents.

Lack of diversity in the library workforce is well documented (Davis and Hall 2007), but the statistics do not discriminate between different kinds of academic institutions. This figure contrasts unfavorably with the fact that at community colleges the faculty are still 15–20 percent nonwhite (Bird and Crumpton 2010; Marshall et al. 2005; Provasnik and Planty 2008). Increasing the diversity of a faculty was shown to increase the recruitment of minorities into colleges by Smith (1999) and a more diverse library presence may be equally helpful, especially in providing information literacy instruction. In the DTCCL, only 7 percent of the respondents identified themselves as nonwhite.

Unique Mission and Governance

Community colleges have multiple missions that affirm their unique nature among postsecondary institutions. It has been acknowledged that community colleges are the primary locus for workforce training and retraining. The Bill and Melinda Gates Foundation is funding research into the methods and programs that work to improve graduation rates in these colleges. In addition, community colleges provide basic skills training, a wide range of community training programs, and recently have added middle and early college programs that are offered to high school students that wish to earn a combined high school–associates degree in a specialty program such as allied health. On the DTCCL, 74 percent of the respondents said that their campus had such a program.

It is difficult for libraries to meet the needs of these workforce classes. On the DTCCL survey, when librarians were asked if their information literacy programs served the needs of vocational classes, 37 percent said no.

Community college libraries are structured differently than those in four-year institutions. They have long had a variety of administrative structures, a situation that began with the change of name to "learning resource centers." As with the commonly used "media center" appellation used in school libraries, the phrase was meant to convey a place where resources beyond books could be found. In addition, in some systems the name came to mean a combination of traditional library functions with more academic success–oriented departments, such as tutoring, testing, and instructional technology. Though these trends are evident in the documentation of job descriptions and organizational charts done by Born, Clayton, and Balash

(2002), this work is not sufficient to inform curriculum development because there is no recommendation on which of these models represents best practice. The DTCCL showed that although 73 percent of the respondents report to the academic affairs department, 20 percent said that they reported to the instructional technology area. It must also be noted that many community college libraries are run by a minimal number of professionally trained staff, sometimes there is only one MLIS in each facility.

Training Needs

The skills needed by librarians in these institutions are not unique, but the degree to which those skills are required can be. Critical areas of focus for training community college librarians are:

- Working with diverse clients. As outlined above, diversity includes nontraditional ages, and great disparities in ability, as well as ethnic, language, and cultural differences due to drawing from first-generation college attendees.

- Workforce and lifelong learning issues. All libraries are centers for lifelong learning, but the learning that happens in community colleges prepares many for education outside of that institution. Community college librarians have to prepare students with sometimes minimal high school preparation for either completing a four-year degree or going to work in a dynamic workplace that demands flexibility and responsiveness.

- Early and Middle Colleges. The challenge of dealing with these younger students at the same time as attending to adult learners' needs makes community college librarianship more allied with public libraries than other academic libraries.

- Distance education programs. Though not unique to community colleges the increase in students taking online coursework presents a critical challenge to community college librarians because there are so few professional librarians on staff. Maintaining face-to-face presence while still providing support to off-campus students can strain any staff, especially when there are so many other responsibilities.

- Small staffs. Unlike in many other postsecondary institutions, librarians have a higher academic degree than many of the faculty and administrators. Yet at the same time, many have only one credentialed librarian. This means that the librarians are called upon to do a broader array of duties than those in four-year institutions. Community college librarians must know everything from acquisitions to systems administration, as well as doing instruction and curriculum design.

From preliminary results on the DTCLC and subsequent focus groups, the need for training might Include:

- Management skills—governance issues, assessment of programs and effectiveness
- Administrative skills—grant writing, advocacy, public relations
- Personal skills—Emotional intelligence, consulting, cultural competence, relationship building
- Adult learning—basic skills students, workforce development students, college transfers

- Distance education support via new technologies
- Collections building in subject areas that librarians have not been educated within
- Workplace information literacy and instructional design

An Acute Need

The DTCCL survey found that 40 percent of the 163 respondents had graduated over 25 years ago from their library program. It corroborated the findings of the Workforce Issues in Library and Information Science (WILIS) project. Funded by IMLS and completed by the University of North Carolina at Chapel Hill (2005–2008), the workforce studied the career patterns of MLIS and MLS graduates from LIS programs in North Carolina. In that study, the number of community college librarians was limited so that all academic librarians were counted together in most published analyses. When the community college librarians were separated in a special analysis of the data,[2] the demographics showed the median age to be 46 for that small sample (N=60). The average number of years since graduation with an MLIS for this group was 16.8 years. This indicates a mid-career or older workforce presently in community college libraries. Anecdotal evidence has indicated that at retirement these librarians are not being replaced by librarians. The survey evidence did indicate that only a small minority of respondents felt they had specific training for the community college library.

Introduction to the Practicum Model in ECCL

The proposed project will use the teaching library model pioneered in New York State under the IMLS funded *Making It Real!* project. The model was first proposed by Suzanne Stauffer (2006) and enhanced by the Teaching Library project at UNCG. It assumes tripartite participation in the learning process (see Figure 1). The practicum supervisor, the LIS faculty supervisor, and the student work together in three intersecting loops or sets. The first set represents practical support to the student through scholarships from the school and mentoring at the libraries. The second set encompasses the student and the LIS program in teaching and learning about the principles and research about librarianship. The third loop is one that is rarely connected, the one between the working professional and the LIS faculty members.

The locus of the grant and the direction by a faculty member would also provide institutional support for the teaching library model. The teaching library practica will be beneficial to the community college staff because they will be exposed to new information that the students are learning in their coursework and support for their role as practicum supervisors. The WILIS study (Marshall et al., 2005) supports the perceived need for training by community college librarians. The DTCCL also

---

[2]The WILIS 1 and 2 studies were supported by grants from the Institute of Museum and Library Services. The primary research team from the School of Information and Library Science at UNC Chapel Hill and the UNC Institute on Aging consisted of: Joanne Gard Marshall, Lead Principal Investigator; Victor W. Marshall, Co-Principal Investigator; Jennifer Craft Morgan, Co-Principal Investigator; Deborah Barreau, Co-Investigator; Barbara Moran, Co-Investigator; Paul Solomon, Co-Investigator; Susan Rathbun Grubb, Research Scientist; Cheryl A. Thompson, Project Manager. Many thanks to them for sharing this unpublished data.

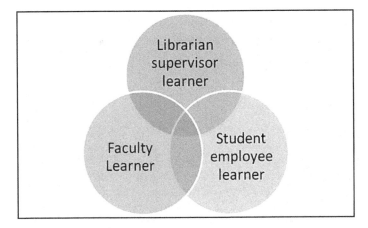

Figure A.1.   Teaching-Librarian-Faculty model of practicum

found that librarians were in need of technology skills. Most said that they had learned things like systems administration, technical troubleshooting, and supervision on the job. Sixty-three percent agreed or strongly agreed with the statement, *Compared to five years ago I feel more pressure to continually learn new skills*, and 72 percent said that they need to perform new tasks. When asked what tasks they needed the most help with, most (75 percent) noted high tech tasks. The respondents to the WILIS study said that it was primarily learning on the job that helped them to keep up to date following their library education. The continuing education modules combined with a teaching library practicum for MLIS students, then, may help to extend the working life of mid-career library professionals so that the drain of experience from librarianship is lessened. At the same time it will provide the hands-on training promoted in service and experiential learning programs.[3]

Intended Results

The intended results from this grant can be summarized in the following table recognizing the background issue, the result expected, and the favorable attribute of the process to be used in the grant:

Background Issue	Result	Favorable Attribute
Lack of diversity in community college librarians (90 percent white)	Librarians ready to serve the diverse community college student population	Recruit diversity candidates from the MLIS student population into the teach-librarian practica
Workforce learners	Training in workplace information literacy	UNCG DLIS has recently launched research into this area
Mid-career training needs	Continuing education modules based on the DACUM model	Identification of needs from constituencies to strengthen community college librarianship

---

[3]See, for example, Roy, L., K. Jensen, and A. H. Meyers. *Service Learning: Linking Library Education and Practice.* Chicago: American Library Association, 2009.

(Continued)

Background Issue	Result	Favorable Attribute
Retirement of CC librarians	MLIS students with strong practicum experiences	Employing the Teaching-Library-Faculty model
Lack of LIS community college research agenda	Involvement of the research team in community college–based issues	Empirical base for research and new knowledge

Impact

The impact of the proposed research and curriculum development will be felt regionally and nationally. IMLS funding will support the following:

1. Impact 1. Librarians will contribute to the national conversation on the centrality of community colleges to lifelong learning and economic development and place the focus on one major component of executing this mission, the community college library.

2. Impact 2. A flexible curriculum that addresses the needs of current and future community college librarians. In turn, these trained librarians will be strong advocates that will ensure that the libraries that they serve are adequately funded within their traditionally underfunded institutions.

3. Impact 3. The teaching library model will foster collaboration and engagement between the academy and community college libraries enhancing the mid-careers of the professionals and furthering the goals of MLIS graduates.

4. Impact 4. Continuing education courses can be offered online and provided both to the 56 community college libraries in North Carolina and nationally. In addition, master's-level coursework can be provided nationally through avenues like the web-based Information Science Education (WISE) consortium (see http://www.wisepedagogy.org/).

5. Impact 5. The effectiveness of the program will be monitored for implementation in other areas of LIS education.

6. Impact 6. The grant provides a platform for development of a working continuing education model housed in an ALA-accredited Library and Information Studies department.

DIVERSITY

Practicum funding will be intended for underrepresented groups in librarianship, according to the May 2009 UNCG LIS Department *Recruitment for Diversity Policy*, which states, "the vibrant variety of human characteristics that combine to shape each one of us. These characteristics include not only the familiar categories of race, ethnicity, gender and sexual orientation, but also: age, cognitive style, disability, economic, educational and geographic background, languages spoken, marital status, political affiliation, religious beliefs. Valuing diversity means recognizing that we are all shaped by numerous and varied factors, making each of us uniquely qualified to contribute to the collective goal." In addition, and importantly for community college librarianship, socioeconomic background will be an important piece of the diversity landscape in this program.

The UNCG Academic and Cultural Enrichment (ACE) Scholars Program with IMLS funding was based on these same ideals and has successfully recruited representatives from these groups into the LIS program. Involvement from those scholars in the recruitment of new students will be encouraged. Similar recruitment efforts would be made in Virginia, where an existing Common Market agreement exists, and with South Carolina near Charlotte, where some students attend the UNCG program based there.

A unique recruitment effort will be made to recruit paraprofessional staff working in community college libraries who are members of underrepresented groups to attend the MLIS program. These staff members already have a commitment to these organizations, and with the financial assistance offered by the grant, they would be perfect candidates to be the professional staff of the future. In this program, diversity is broadly defined. The goal is not mere representation of different backgrounds, but ability to engage effectively with a broad constituency.

PROJECT DESIGN AND EVALUATION

The goals of the program will be reached with the collaboration and participation of the Advisory Board, Michael Crumpton from the UNCG Jackson Library; Beth Martin, LIS faculty member and Charlotte coordinator; and the DLIS faculty. The design and evaluation of each goal in the project are described below.

Goal 1. Developing a series of continuing education modules specifically for 21st-century community college librarians based on research and situated within the MLIS program.

Design. Focus groups will be held in conjunction with the North Carolina Library Association annual conference to begin the design of three DACUM (Developing A Curriculum) meetings. DACUM is a storyboarding process that we will use to provide a snapshot of what a librarian does in a community college environment. The results will be used to design continuing education modules for practicing librarians, training for practicum supervisors in community college libraries, and then MLIS coursework.

Evaluation. Learning outcomes for the continuing education modules will be developed from the DACUM process. Assessments of the learning outcomes will be done before and after the coursework is completed.

Goal 2. Employing a Teaching-Librarian-Faculty practicum in participating community colleges to prepare new MLIS graduates and to enhance the careers of practicing librarians.

Design. Practica students will be placed in partner community college libraries. In the second and third year, the MLIS candidates will be mentored through a specifically designed practicum course at appropriate community colleges in the area using the teaching library model. The staff in each participating library will be partners with LIS faculty and the students in creating a rich library experience focused on professional development.

Evaluation. Participants will use self-monitoring techniques to document their experiences, which will be analyzed for evidence of personal and professional growth and learning. The librarian supervisors will provide similar documentation about their experience as participants in the teaching library practica, and they will also reflect on their interaction with the LIS faculty and about their own learning. The librarian supervisors will do a formal evaluation of the MLIS candidates work. All of this evidence will be analyzed in order to strengthen the practicum experience and the curriculum by the faculty mentors. It will also be documented in appropriate ways and disseminated through the plan outlined below.

Goal 3. Curriculum for MLIS students.
   Design. The continuing education modules will be developed in online course-ware that can be combined and enhanced to serve as the basis for full 3-credit-hour course development with similar learning outcomes that will be incorporated into the MLIS curriculum and offered nationally through the WISE consortium.
   Evaluation. In addition to the traditional course evaluations undertaken by the DLIS, additional evaluation of the impact on the community college libraries will be done through practicum supervisors and employers who hire MLIS graduates.

Goal 4. Textbook that trains future CC librarians and helps practicing CC librarians to update their skills.
   Design. A textbook in a variety of formats and built from materials in the continuing education modules and the curriculum will be created to provide sustainability for the project.
   Evaluation. The sales and use of this book for ongoing professional development will be the ultimate evaluation

PROJECT RESOURCES

The requested funds will be added to the cost-sharing resources from the UNCG School of Education and the University Libraries and will be used to reach the goals of the project. The majority of these resources will be devoted to the practitioner participants, the practicum student participants, and the master's student assistant. The members of the community college community that attend the DACUM meetings will receive a small award for their time and sharing. A small percentage is used for conference travel for the principal investigators to disseminate the results of the program.

PERSONNEL

The project team will ensure the success of the program. **Dr. Nora Bird** (Assistant Professor and principal investigator). She will oversee the project and write the reports to IMLS. She will oversee the work of the master's student working with the project, develop the coursework, and supervise the practica. She will devote 10 percent of her time during all three summers of the project and 30 percent of her time during the academic years. **Mr. Michael Crumpton**, MLS, Assistant Dean of Administrative Services, UNCG University Libraries and former director of the Wake Tech Community College, will be co-principal investigator, a liaison to the community college librarians, and work with them at 10 percent of his time. **Ms. Sarah Elizabeth Martin**, Clinical Faculty Member in the Library and Information Studies Department, will work on course development and practicum placements, and **Dr. Clara Chu**, Professor and Chair, Library and Information Studies Department, will supervise the expenditure of funds, oversee continuity, and lead the evaluation at 5 percent of her time. Master's student will be recruited from MLIS candidates, and be an assistant to the project manager.

Partners and collaborators from the field have been identified, and letters of support are included in an appendix. They are: Central Piedmont Community College, Davidson County Community College, Guilford County Community Technical College, Wake Tech Community College, Wilkes County Community College, the State Library of North Carolina, and the State Library of South Carolina. This team of collaborators will form an Advisory Board to the program managers and the community college libraries.

MANAGEMENT PLAN

The grant period runs from July 1, 2011 to June 30, 2014. Throughout the period the principal investigator and project manager will meet with advisory board members. Evaluation activities will take place at each stage of the grant process. Tasks to be completed for each quarter are listed below:

2011–2012

- Quarter 1 (July–Sept 2011): Confirm Advisory Board participants; hire and train Master's student GA; add grant activities to the website; develop DACUM framework and evaluation.

- Quarter 2 (Oct–Dec 2011): Invite attendees to the North Carolina Library Association pre-conference; Distribute surveys and DACUM information; Schedule DACUM workshops; Plan Advisory Board meetings.

- Quarter 3 (Jan–Mar 2012): Gather and analyze survey and DACUM information; Lead DACUM workshops.

- Quarter 4 (Apr–Jun 2012): Begin recruiting; Meet with Advisory Board to review progress and plan for the next two quarters; Create 2 continuing education modules.

2012–2013

- Quarter 1 (July–Sept 2012): Meet with Advisory Board to plan activities for the coming year; Present results of surveys and DACUM at national conferences; Implement pilot continuing education modules and analyze course feedback; assess and evaulate continuing education modules; Training of the practicum supervisors; Recruit MLIS students to work in the first classes

- Quarter 2 (Oct–Dec 2012): Implement first practicums with course credit; Initiate teach practicum model

- Quarter 3 (Jan–Mar 2013): Implement first paid practicum; Meet with Advisory Board members to review the results from the first class; Meet with the trained practicum supervisors to evaluate the practicums; Distribute evaluations

- Quarter 4 (Apr–June 2013): Complete first teaching of the experimental LIS688 community college course; Complete the syllabi for all coursework for the Fall 2013 semester

2013–2014

- Quarter 1 (July–Sept 2013): Place course descriptions into UNCG Curriculum Review process; Complete matching of teacher library practica with students and community college library; Meet with Advisory Board to match MLIS candidate with institution; Examine projects and coursework completed by the pilot group

- Quarter 2 (Oct–Dec 2013): Supervise and document practica; Begin documentation for textbook and find publisher if applicable
- Quarter 3 (Jan–Mar 2014): Complete the evaluation of the placements and assess impact on mid-career librarians; Meet with Advisory Board to plan the last quarter of the grant
- Quarter 4 (Apr–June 2014): Complete evaluation and final report

COMMUNICATION PLAN

The intended results from this study suggest many venues for dissemination. The principal investigators will establish an interactive website that will build throughout the length of the project with student input, collaborator input, and published results. The primary mode of communication will be with the members of the Advisory Board and the larger community college community through the informal communication channels of a dedicated website and blog written by the principal investigator. Dissemination to more formal conferences would be to:

- Website, *Defining the Community College Librarian:* https://sites.google.com/a/uncg.edu/cc-librarian-project/
- National Council for Learning Resources, a division of the American Association of Community Colleges that publishes a journal entitled *Community College Journal*, will be a focus for dissemination.
- State Library Association Conferences in North Carolina, South Carolina, and Virginia in 2011, 2012, and 2013.
- Association for Library and Information Science Education (ALISE), January 2012, 2013, 2014
- North Carolina Community College Learning Resources Association, including American Library Association in summer 2011, 2012, 2013, and 2014.

The principal investigators will all be involved in presentation and writing about this work. Papers will be submitted to peer-reviewed journals such as *College and Research Libraries, Library Trends, and Library and Information Science Research.*

In addition, the continuing education modules and resultant coursework will be its own dissemination tool. The coursework will be developed for online delivery and could be offered nationally through the WISE consortium. In addition, a post–master's certificate will be considered and could be offered through the same venue and at UNCG.

SUSTAINABILITY

The continuing education modules can be offered to other participants for a small fee during and after the grant. The developed coursework will be filed with the appropriate University administrators and accrediting agencies. The courses can then become a permanent addition to the UNCG offerings with faculty support provided by Dr. Nora Bird. The research agenda for the principal investigators, in collaboration with partner libraries and the MLIS candidates, will promote continual relevance to the field. The documentation of the teaching library practicum model may lead to other successful implementations of these throughout the library field. It will certainly strengthen the implementation of such practica within the UNCG LIS program. The planned textbook can be the foundation of course adoption in other LIS programs and the continual renewal of practicing librarians' skill set.

The practica offered through the grant will sustain and promote the careers of the project-funded students for many years. They will build a network of support for community college libraries throughout higher education.

REFERENCES

Bill & Melinda Gates Foundation. (June 22, 2009). Community Colleges and States Selected to Boost College Graduation Rates by Improving Remedial Courses and Strategies. Retrieved from http://www.gatesfoundation.org/press-releases/Pages/raising-graduation-rates-community-colleges-090622.aspx

Dowell, D. (2006). Introduction. In D. Dowell (Ed.) *It's All about Student Learning: Managing Community and Other College Libraries in the 21st Century*. Westport, CT: Libraries Unlimited.

Karp, R. (2006). Leadership Issues for Community College Librarians. In D. Dowell (Ed.) *It's All about Student Learning: Managing Community and Other College Libraries in the 21st Century*. Westport, CT: Libraries Unlimited.

Marshall, J. G., Marshall, V. W., Morgan, J. C., Barreau, D., Moran, B. B., Solomon, P., et al. (2005). *Workforce Issues in Library and Information Science (WILIS)*. UNC Institute on Aging and UNC School of Information and Library Science: Institute of Museum and Library Services.

Provasnik, S. and Planty, M. (2008). *Community Colleges: Special Supplement to the Condition of Education. Statistical Analysis Report*. Washington, DC: National Center for Education Statistics.

Smith, S. (1999). Working Recruitment Miracles. *Black Issues in Higher Education 16* (170), 40–41.

Stauffer, S. (2006, November). *A Framework for a "Teaching Library": A Preliminary Study*. Paper presented at the NYLA Annual Conference, Saratoga Springs, NY.

Release from the White House summit. White House. Office of the Press Secretary. (July 14, 2009). Below are excerpts of the President's remarks in Warren, Michigan, today and a fact sheet on the American Graduation Initiative. Retrieved from http://www.whitehouse.gov/the_press_office/Excerpts-of-the-Presidents-remarks-in-Warren-Michigan-and-fact-sheet-on-the-American-Graduation-Initiative/

Appendix B

THE 21ST-CENTURY COMMUNITY COLLEGE LIBRARIAN SURVEY RESULTS

Please indicate your gender.

Answer Options	Response Percent	Response Count
Male	18.7%	35
Female	81.3%	152
prefer not to answer	0.0%	0
	answered question	187
	skipped question	3

Which one of the following census categories best describes your racial or ethnic background?

Answer Options	Response Percent	Response Count
White	90.3%	167
Black, African American, or Negro	3.8%	7
American Indian or Alaska Native	0.0%	0
Asian Indian	0.5%	1
Asian (Chinese, Japanese, Korean, Vietnamese)	2.7%	5
Prefer not to answer	2.7%	5
Other (please specify)		2
	answered question	185
	skipped question	5

What degrees or training do you have for the position that you hold?

Answer Options	Response Percent	Response Count
MLIS or MLS or equivalent ALA-accredited degree	98.9%	181
A bachelor's degree with some Library Tech training	2.7%	5

(continued)

154 APPENDIX B

(Continued)

What degrees or training do you have for the position that you hold?

Answer Options	Response Percent	Response Count
A bachelor's degree in information technology or instructional technology	0.0%	0
A master's degree in instructional technology	2.2%	4
An associate's degree in information technology	0.0%	0
An associate's degree in technical or public services	0.5%	1
Other (please specify)		19
	answered question	183
	skipped question	7

When did you receive your last degree?

Answer Options	Response Percent	Response Count
Within the last 5 years	31.1%	48
Within the last 10 years	28.5%	43
Within the last 15 years	16.6%	26
Within the last 25 years	23.8%	37
Over 25		
Other (please specify)		
	answered question	151
	skipped question	39

Did you take any courses during your coursework specifically targeted at Community College Librarianship or work in Community College administration?

Answer Options	Response Percent	Response Count
Yes	8.2%	15
No	91.8%	168
Other (please specify)		8
	answered question	183
	skipped question	7

What skills have you learned on the job versus in your academic training?

Answer Options	Response Percent	Response Count
Google Master	47.7%	82
Social networking	66.3%	114
Technical troubleshooter	76.7%	132
Systems administration	38.4%	66
Supervision	65.7%	113

(Continued)

What skills have you learned on the job versus in your academic training?

Answer Options	Response Percent	Response Count
Other (please specify)		30
answered question		172
skipped question		18

Do you speak any of the following languages? Choose any that apply.

Answer Options	Response Percent	Response Count
Spanish	55.0%	33
Vietnamese	0.0%	0
French	36.7%	22
German	15.0%	9
Russian	5.0%	3
Chinese	8.3%	5
Other (please specify)		15
answered question		60
skipped question		130

Within what administrative division does the library report?

Answer Options	Response Percent	Response Count
Academic affairs	72.6%	122
Student affairs/services	5.4%	9
Instructional/Learning technology	20.8%	35
Business services	1.2%	2
Other (please specify)		20
answered question		168
skipped question		22

Is there a middle college, early college, or other high school/college program based at your community college?

Answer Options	Response Percent	Response Count
Middle college	17.8%	28
Early college	52.9%	83
No	33.1%	52
Other (please specify)		35
answered question		157
skipped question		33

If you answered yes to the question above, do you provide library services to these students?

Answer Options	Response Percent	Response Count
Yes	95.2%	120
No	4.8%	6
Other (please specify)		5
	answered question	126
	skipped question	64

Does your community college offer online classes?

Answer Options	Response Percent	Response Count
Yes	99.5%	183
No	0.5%	1
Other (please specify)		0
	answered question	184
	skipped question	6

If your community college offers online classes, how do you provide information literacy instruction to those students?

Answer Options	Response Percent	Response Count
Through online tutorials	81.6%	142
Through online live webinars through net meeting, Elluminate or other systems	8.0%	14
Phone chat or comparable	46.0%	80
Remote seated sessions	7.5%	13
None at this time	12.6%	22
Other (please specify)		41
	answered question	174
	skipped question	16

Please estimate what percentage of your users are guided to the library, or LRC, by their instructors or through their programs?

Answer Options	Response Percent	Response Count
0–10%	4.0%	7
11–25%	35.8%	63
26–50%	32.4%	57
51–75%	21.6%	38
76–100%	6.3%	11
Other (please specify)		11
	answered question	176
	skipped question	14

What are the top three skills that you would like a new employee to possess? Choose three from the following list:

Answer Options	1	2	3	Response Count
Website creation	8	18	25	51
Social networking and marketing	6	21	47	74
Bibliographic database usage	33	50	20	103
Database creation	1	2	5	8
Digitization	3	7	3	13
Teaching/information literacy experience	107	39	9	155
Project management	4	22	30	56
Other (please specify)				28
		answered question		163
		skipped question		27

Are your library instructional classes different for core education/transfer/college prep courses from technology or vocation-related courses?

Answer Options	Response Percent	Response Count
Yes	63.3%	95
No	36.7%	55
Other (please specify)		29
	answered question	150
	skipped question	40

Please estimate the percentage of your library instructional program or efforts provided for core education/transfer/college prep courses in comparison to overall instruction.

Answer Options	Response Percent	Response Count
0–10%	9.7%	16
11–25%	11.5%	19
26–50%	15.2%	25
51–75%	25.5%	42
76–100%	38.2%	63
Other (please specify)		3
	answered question	165
	skipped question	25

Please estimate the percentage of your library instructional program or efforts provided for technology or vocational courses in comparison to overall instruction.

Answer Options	Response Percent	Response Count
0–10%	46.0%	75
11–25%	39.9%	65

(continued)

(Continued)

Please estimate the percentage of your library instructional program or efforts provided for technology or vocational courses in comparison to overall instruction.

Answer Options	Response Percent	Response Count
26–50%	9.2%	15
51–75%	2.5%	4
76–100%	2.5%	4
Other (please specify)		6
	answered question	163
	skipped question	27

Which of the following skills do you cover in your core education/transfer/college prep IL classes? Choose the top three.

Answer Options	1	2	3	Response Count
Evaluating resources	70	60	21	151
Citation writing	19	31	47	97
Plagiarism	8	10	27	45
Special resources for the topic	82	44	14	140
Using Advanced Google options	2	1	8	11
Using citation software such as Endnote or Zotero	2	2	7	11
Learning about career trends or information on workforce influences	2	2	10	14
Other (please specify)				34
		answered question		162
		skipped question		28

Which of the following skills do you cover in your technology or vocation related IL classes? Choose the top three.

Answer Options	1	2	3	Rating Average	Response Count
Evaluating resources	52	38	33	1.85	123
Citation writing	7	21	31	2.41	59
Plagiarism	4	12	13	2.31	29
Special resources for the topic	75	48	8	1.49	131
Using Advanced Google options	1	4	12	2.65	17

(Continued)

Which of the following skills do you cover in your technology or vocation related IL classes? Choose the top three.

Answer Options	1	2	3	Rating Average	Response Count
Using citation software such as Endnote or Zotero	2	0	7	2.56	9
Learning about career trends or information on workforce influences	5	19	25	2.41	49
Other (please specify)					28
			answered question		151
			skipped question		39

Please identify criteria for selecting resources related to supporting core education/transfer/college prep courses. Choose all that apply.

Answer Options	Response Percent	Response Count
Expense	67.9%	110
Use in next-level institutions	16.7%	27
Recommendation of faculty	79.0%	128
Currency	68.5%	111
Relevance to coursework	91.4%	148
Relevant to professional or subject major	62.3%	101
Other (please specify)		8
	answered question	162
	skipped question	28

Please identify criteria for selecting resources related to supporting technical or vocation-based courses. Choose all that apply.

Answer Options	Response Percent	Response Count
Expense	65.6%	103
Use in next-level institutions	9.6%	15
Recommendation of faculty	82.8%	130
Currency	69.4%	109
Relevance to coursework	89.2%	140
Relevant to professional or subject major	61.8%	97
Other (please specify)		3
	answered question	157
	skipped question	33

The primary objectives for your instructional classes for core education/transfer/ college prep courses are:

Answer Options	Response Percent	Response Count
To write research paper	30.8%	49
To gain job understanding	0.6%	1
To learn more about profession or subject major	0.0%	0
To support instructor's objectives	42.8%	68
Demonstrate use of library databases	25.8%	41
Other (please specify)		11
	answered question	159
	skipped question	31

The primary objectives for your instructional classes for technical or vocational courses are:

Answer Options	Response Percent	Response Count
To write research paper	9.7%	15
To gain job understanding	4.5%	7
To learn more about profession or subject major	15.6%	24
To support instructor's objectives	52.6%	81
Demonstrate use of library databases	17.5%	27
	answered question	154
	skipped question	36

REFERENCES

Abels, Eileen G. n.d. "Information Seeking Behavior and the Generations." http://
www.ala.org/rusa/sites/ala.org.rusa/files/content/sections/rss/rsssection/
rsscomm/virtualreferencecommittee/an07infoseekgen.pdf .

"About—Big6." 2012. *The Big 6 Tm: Information and Technology Skills for Student Success.*
Accessed July 25. http://big6.com/pages/about.php.

ACRL Racial and Ethnic Diversity Committee. 2012. "Diversity Standards: Cultural Competency Standards for Academic Librarians: Approved by the ACRL Board of Directors,
April 2012." *College and Research Libraries News* 73, no. 9: 551–61.

Agosto, Denise E., Lily Rozaklis, Craig MacDonald, and Eileen G. Abels. 2011. "A Model of
the Reference and Information Service Process." *Reference & User Services Quarterly*
50, no. 3 (March 1): 235–44.

Aldrich, Alan W. 2011. "Judging Books by Their Covers: Managing the Tensions between
Paperback and Clothbound Purchases in Academic Libraries." *College & Research
Libraries* 70, no. 1: 57–70.

Alire, Camila A. 2007. "Emotional Intelligence and Diversity in Academic Libraries." In
Academic Librarians as Emotionally Intelligent Leaders, by Peter Hernon, Joan
Giesecke, and Camila A. Alire. Westport, CT: Libraries Unlimited.

American Association of Community Colleges. 2003. "AACC Position Statement on Library
and Learning Resource Center Programs," http://www.aacc.nche.edu/About/
Positions/Pages/ps01062003.aspx.

American Association of Community Colleges. 2008. "AACC Position Statement on Information Literacy." http://www.aacc.nche.edu/about/positions/pages/ps0505
2008.aspx.

American Association of Community Colleges . 2012. *Reclaiming the American Dream: A
Report from the 21st Century Commission on the Future of Community Colleges.* http://
www.aacc.nche.edu/aboutcc/21stcenturyreport/21stCenturyReport.pdf.

American Association of Community Colleges. 2011. *AACCs Commitment to Diversity,
Inclusion, and Equity.* http://www.aacc.nche.edu/Resources/aaccprograms/
diversity/Documents/diversity_commitment.pdf.

American Association of Community Colleges. n.d. "Fast Facts." http://www.aacc.nche.edu/
AboutCC/Pages/fastfacts.aspx.

American Association of Community Colleges. 2005. "Position Statement on Student Services and Library and Learning Resource Center Program Support for Distributed Learning." http://www.aacc.nche.edu/About/Positions/Pages/ps02102005.aspx.

American Library Association. Association of College and Research Libraries. *Presidential Committee on Information Literacy.* Washington, DC. http://www.ala.org/ala/mgrps/divs/acrl/publications/whitepapers/presidential.cfm.

American Library Association. Office of Diversity. 2012. "Diversity Counts Tables. http://www.ala.org/offices/sites/ala.org.offices/files/content/diversity/diversitycounts/diversitycountstables2012.pdf.

Amsberry, Dawn. 2008. "Talking the Talk: Library Classroom Communication and International Students." *The Journal of Academic Librarianship* 34, no. 4 (July): 354–57. doi:10.1016/j.acalib.2008.05.007.

Antell, Karen, 2004. "Why Do College Students Use Public Libraries? A Phenomenological Study." *Reference & User Services Quarterly* 43, no. 3: 227–36.

Arnold, Jennifer. 2010. "The Community College Conundrum: Workforce Issues in Community College Libraries." *Library Trends* 59, no. 1–2: 220–36. doi:10.1353/lib.2010.0033.

Association of College and Research Libraries. 2011. "Standards for Libraries in Higher Education." http://www.ala.org/acrl/standards/standardslibraries.

Austenfeld, Anne Marie. 2009. "Building the College Library Collection to Support Curriculum Growth." *Collection Management* 34, no. 3: 209–27. doi:10.1080/01462670902975027.

Auyeung, Shuk-chun and Don Hausrath. 1998. "Information Competency Plan for the California Community Colleges." http://www.santarosa.edu/kathy/ICC/bog98-9.html.

Bakamitsos, George A., and George J. Siomkos. 2004. "Context Effects in Marketing Practice." *Journal of Consumer Behavior* 3: 304–14.

Beal, Vangie. 2012. "5 Free Open Source Alternatives to Microsoft Office." *PCWorld* . http://www.pcworld.com/article/2010005/5-free-open-source-alternatives-to-microsoft-office.html.

Beaudry, Richard. "Transition Literacy in High Schools—A School Model." http://www.acsu.buffalo.edu/~as347/transitionliteracy.pdf.

Bell, Dorothy, and Betty Jo Gaston. 2005. "Collection Development." *Community & Junior College Libraries* 12, no. 3: 9–16. doi:10.1300/J107v12n03_04.

Bird, Nora J., Michael Crumpton, Melynda Ozan, and Tim Williams. 2012. "Workplace Information Literacy: A Neglected Priority for Community College Libraries." *Journal of Business & Finance Librarianship* 17, no. 1: 18–33. doi:10.1080/08963568.2012.630593.

Bird, Nora J. and Williams, Tim. (October 4, 2012). "Making Sense of Different Workplaces: Using O*NET to Inform Design of Information Literacy Instruction. Presented at the Library 2.012 online conference. Recording available at https://sas.elluminate.com/site/external/recording/playback/link/table/dropin?sid=2008350&suid=D.4F374F7BB9FA0DA59D3934C3618B61.

Bock, D. Joleen. 1984. "From Libraries to Learning Resources: Six Decades of Progress—And Still Changing." *Community & Junior College Libraries* 3, no. 2: 35–46.

Boggs, George R. "Democracy's Colleges: The Evolution of the Community College in America." http://www.aacc.nche.edu/AboutCC/whsummit/Documents/boggs_whsummitbrief.pdf.

Booth, Char, Barbara T. Mates, Christopher S. Guder, S. G. Ranti Junus, Debra A. Riley-Huff, Jennifer Tatomir, and Joanna Tatomir. 2012. *Making Libraries Accessible: Adaptive Design and Assistive Technology.* Chicago: ALA TechSource,

Bopp, Richard E., and Linda C. Smith. 2011. *Reference and Information Services: An Introduction.* 4th ed. Santa Barbara, CA: Libraries Unlimited.

Born, Judy, Sue Clayton, and Aggie Balash. 2000. *Community College Library Job Descriptions and Organizational Charts.* Chicago: Community and Junior College Library Section, Association of College and Research Libraries.

Bostick, Sharon Lee. 1992. "The Development and Validation of the Library Anxiety Scale." PhD dissertation. Wayne State University.

Bradberry, Travis, and Jean Greaves. 2009. *Emotional Intelligence 2.0.* San Diego: TalentSmart.

Branin, Joseph J. 2009. "The Use of Library Material." *College & Research Libraries* 70: 311–12.

Breivik, Patricia Senn. 1998. *Student Learning in the Information Age.* Phoenix: American Council on Education/Oryx Press.

Brown, Mary E, and Rebecca Power. 2006. *Exhibits in Libraries: A Practical Guide.* Jefferson, NC: McFarland.

Bruce, Christine. 2008. *Informed Learning.* Chicago: Association of College and Research Libraries.

Budd, John. 2009. *Framing Library Instruction.* Chicago: Association of College and Research Libraries.

Capital Community College. n.d. "A Capital History." *Capital Community College.* http://www.ccc.commnet.edu/history.htm.

Carnegie Foundation for the Advancement of Teaching. Lookup & Listings: Standard Listings. http://classifications.carnegiefoundation.org.

Carr, David. 2002. "A Community Mind." *Public Libraries* 41, no. 5: 284.

Case, Donald Owen. 2002. *Looking for Information: A Survey of Research on Information Seeking, Needs, and Behavior.* San Diego: Academic Press.

Cassell, Kay Ann, and Uma Hiremath. 2011. *Reference and Information Services in the 21st Century: An Introduction,* 2nd ed. revised. Chicago: Neal-Schuman Publishers.

"Center for Media Literacy." 2012. http://www.medialit.org/.

Certo, Samuel C. 2013. *Supervision: Concepts and Skill-Building.* New York: McGraw-Hill Irwin.

Choy, Susan. 2002. "Findings From the Condition of Education 2002: Nontraditional Undergraduates." *National Center for Education Statistics.* August. http://nces.ed.gov/pubs2002/2002012.pdf.

Chu, Clara M. November 2004. "Raison D'être for Multicultural Library Services." *IFLA Library Services to Multicultural Populations Section Newsletter.*

CMS Critic. "Huge List of Content Management Systems (List of CMS Software)." *CMS Critic.* http://www.cmscritic.com/resource-lists/cms-list/.

Cohen, Arthur M., and Florence B. Brawer. 2008. *The American Community College.* 5th ed. San Francisco: Jossey-Bass.

Committee on Information Technology Literacy, National Research Council. 1999. *Being Fluent with Information Technology.* Washington, DC: National Academies Press.

Connors, Roger, and Tom Smith. 2011. *Change the Culture, Change the Game: The Breakthrough Strategy for Energizing Your Organization and Creating Accountability for Results.* New York: Portfolio Penguin.

Cook, Douglas, and Ryan Sittler. 2008. *Practical Pedagogy for Library Instructors: 17 Innovative Strategies to Improve Student Learning.* Chicago: Association of College and Research Libraries.

Cooper, Jewell E., Ye He, and Barbara B. Levin. 2011. *Developing Critical Cultural Competence: A Guide for 21st-Century Educators.* Thousand Oaks, CA: Corwin Press.

Cooper, Robert K. 1997. "Applying Emotional Intelligence in the Workplace." *Training and Development* 51, no. 12: 31–38.

Cooper, Tab W., and Lucia Stretcher Sigmar. 2012. "Constructive Supervisory Confrontation: What Employees Want." *International Journal of Management & Information Systems* 16: 255–64.

Covey, Stephen R, A. Roger Merrill, and Rebecca R Merrill. 1999. *First Things First: To Live, to Love, to Learn, to Leave a Legacy.* London: Simon & Schuster.

Crandall, JoAnn, and Kent Sheppard. 2004. Adult ESL and the Community College. New York: Council for Advancement of Adult Literacy. http://caalusa.org/eslreport.pdf.

Cross, Terry L., Marva P. Benjamin, Mareasa R. Isaacs, Portland State University, Research and Training Center to Improve Services for Seriously Emotionally Handicapped Children and Their Families, and CASSP Technical Assistance Center. 1989. *Towards a Culturally Competent System of Care.* Washington, DC: CASSP Technical Assistance Center, Georgetown University Child Development Center.

Crumpton, Michael. 2008. "Sounding Off about Noise." *Community and Junior College Libraries* 13, no. 1: 93–103.

Davis, D. and Hall, T. 2007. "Diversity Counts." Chicago: American Library Association Office for Research and Statistics and Office for Diversity.

Davis, Jeff. 2010. *The First-Generation Student Experience: Implications for Campus Practice, and Strategies for Improving Persistence and Success.* Sterling, VA: Stylus Publishing.

De Rosa, Cathy, Joanne Cantrell, Matthew Carlson, Margaret Gallagher, Janet Hawk, Charlotte Sturtz, Brad Gauder, et al. 2011. *Perceptions of Libraries, 2010: Context and Community: A Report to the OCLC Membership.* Dublin, OH: OCLC. http://www.oclc.org/au/en/reports/2010perceptions.htm.

DesMarais, Christina. 2011. "Seven Free Alternatives to Microsoft Office—Techlicious." http://www.techlicious.com/guide/seven-free-alternatives-to-microsoft-office/.

Detmering, Robert, and Claudene Sproles. 2012. "Reference in Transition: A Case Study in Reference Collection Development." *Collection Building* 31: 19–22. doi:10.1108/01604951211199146.

Dinkins, Debbi. 2003. "Circulation as Assessment: Collection Development Policies Evaluated in Terms of Circulation at a Small Academic Library." *College & Research Libraries* 64, no. 1 (January): 46–53.

Dooley, Kim E., James R. Lindner, and Larry McCoy Dooley. 2005. *Advanced Methods in Distance Education: Applications and Practices for Educators, Administrators, and Learners.* Hershey, PA: Information Science.

Dosa, Marta L, and ERIC Clearinghouse on Information Resources. 1977. *Information Counseling: The Best of ERIC.* Syracuse, NY: ERIC Clearinghouse on Information Resources, Syracuse University, School of Education.

Dowell, D. 2006. *It's All about Student Learning: Managing Community and Other College Libraries in the 21st Century.* Westport, CT: Libraries Unlimited.

Dubicki, Eleonora. 2011. *Strategic Planning in College Libraries.* Chicago: College Library Information Packet Committee, College Libraries Section, Association of College and Research Libraries.

Durrance, Joan C. 1995. "Factors That Influence Reference Success: What Makes Questioners Willing to Return." *Reference Librarian*, no. 49/50: 243–65.

Elsner, Paul A, George R Boggs, and Judith T Irwin. 2008. *Global Development of Community Colleges, Technical Colleges, and Further Education Programs.* Washington, DC: Community College Press.

Evans, G. Edward, and Margaret Zarnosky Saponaro. 2005. *Developing Library and Information Center Collections.* Westport, CT: Libraries Unlimited, 2005.

Fantini, Alvino. "Assessment Tools of Intercultural Communicative Competence." http://www.sit.edu/SITOccasionalPapers/feil_appendix_f.pdf.

Fisher, John M. 2005. "A Time for Change?" *Human Resource Development International* 8, no. 2: 257–63. doi:10.1080/13678860500100665.

Fisher, Karen E, Sanda Erdelez, and Lynne McKechnie. 2005. *Theories of Information Behavior.* Medford, NJ: Published for the American Society for Information Science and Technology by Information Today.

Fohl, Claire. 2002. "Weeding." *Community & Junior College Libraries* 10: 47–50. doi:10.1300/J107v10n03_06.

Foster, Nancy Fried, and Susan Gibbons. 2007. *Studying Students: The Undergraduate Research Project at the University of Rochester*. Chicago: Association of College and Research Libraries.

Francis, Mary. 2012. "Weeding the Reference Collection: A Case Study of Collection Management." *The Reference Librarian* 53: 219–234. doi:10.1080/02763877.2011 .619458.

Freire, Paulo. 2000. *Pedagogy of the Oppressed*. New York: Continuum, 2000.

Freire, Paulo, and Ana Maria Araújo Freire. 1994. *Pedagogy of Hope: Reliving Pedagogy of the Oppressed*. New York: Continuum.

Giesecke, Joan, and Beth McNeil. 1999. "Core Competencies and the Learning Organization." *Library Administration & Management* 13, no. 3: 158.

Goleman, Daniel. 1995. *Emotional Intelligence*. New York: Bantam Books.

Gradowski, Gail, Loanne Snavely, Paula Dempsey, and Association of College and Research Libraries. Instruction Section. Teaching Methods Committee. 1998. *Designs for Active Learning: A Sourcebook of Classroom Strategies for Information Education*. Chicago: The Association.

Graham, Warren Davis. 2012. *The Black Belt Librarian: Real-World Safety & Security*. Chicago: American Library Association.

Grassian, Esther S., and Joan R. Kaplowitz. 2009. *Information Literacy Instruction: Theory and Practice*. New York: Neal-Schuman Publishers.

Green, Jen. 2010. "Millennials at Work: Re-imaging Communication in Order to Improve Training." In *Visual Resources Association Bulletin*, 37: 52–54.

Gross, Melissa, and Don Latham. 2012. "What's Skill Got to Do with It? Information Literacy Skills and Self-Views of Ability among First-Year College Students." *Journal of the American Society for Information Science and Technology* 63, no. 3: 574–83.

Hamer, Judah S. 2003. "Coming-Out: Gay Males' Information Seeking." *School Libraries Worldwide* 9, no. 2 (July): 73–89.

Head, Alison J., and Michael Eisenberg. 2010. "Truth Be Told How College Students Evaluate and Use Information in the Digital Age," http://bibpurl.oclc.org/web/40870 http://projectinfolit.org/pdfs/PIL_Fall2010_Survey_FullReport1.pdf.

Heinström, Jannica. 2010. *From Fear to Flow: Personality and Information Reactions*. Oxford: Chandos.

Hernon, Peter, and Charles R. McClure. 1987. *Unobtrusive Testing and Library Reference Services*. Norwood, NJ: Ablex Publishing.

Heu, N. A., and W. N. Nelson. 2009. "A Library Compliance Strategy for Regional Accreditation Standards: Using ACRL Higher Education Standards with Community and Junior Colleges in the Western Association of Schools and Colleges." *College and Undergraduate Libraries* 16: 250–77.

Hook, Sheril. 2012. "Impact? What Three Years of Research Tell Us about Library Instruction." *College & Research Libraries* 73, no.1: 7–10.

Holleman, Peggy. 1989. "Professional Ethics and Community College Librarians." *Community & Junior College Libraries* 6, no. 2: 1–7.

Horton, Forest Woody Jr. 2008. *Understanding Information Literacy: A Primer*. UNESCO Communication and Information Sector. http://www.uis.unesco.org/Communication/ Documents/157020E.pdf .

"Institute of Learning Styles Research." *Overview of the Seven Perceptual Styles*. June 24, 2013. http://www.learningstyles.org/index.html.

Instructional Design Central. "Instructional Design Models and Methods." *Instructional Design Central*. http://www.instructionaldesigncentral.com/htm/IDC_instructional designmodels.htm.

Jiao, Qun G., and Anthony J. Onwuegbuzie. 1997. "Antecedents of Library Anxiety." *Library Quarterly* 67, no. 4: 372–89.

Jiao, Qun G., Anthony J. Onwuegbuzie, and Art A. Lichtenstein. "Library Anxiety: Characteristics of 'At-Risk' College Students." *Library & Information Science Research* 18, no. 2: 151–63.

Jones-Kavalier, Barbara, and Suzanne L. Flannigan. "Connecting the Digital Dots: Literacy of the 21st Century (EDUCAUSE Quarterly) | EDUCAUSE.edu." http://www.educause.edu/ero/article/connecting-digital-dots-literacy-21st-century.

Kahn, Miriam. 2008. *The Library Security and Safety Guide to Prevention, Planning, and Response.* Chicago: American Library Association.

Kalick, Rosanne. 1992. *Community College Libraries: Centers for Lifelong Learning.* Metuchen, NJ: Scarecrow Press.

Katz, William A. 2002. *Introduction to Reference Work.* 8th ed. New York: McGraw-Hill.

Kelley, Michael. 2012. "Coming into Focus: Web-Scale Discovery Services Face Growing Need for Best Practices." *Library Journal* 137, no. 17: 34–40.

Kelly, Robert. 2006. "An Analysis of the Collections at JFK Library: A Case Study." In *It's All about Student Learning: Managing Community and Other College Libraries in the 21st Century,* edited by David Dowell. Westport, CT: Libraries Unlimited.

Kemp, Sid. 2005. *Ultimate Guide to Project Management for Small Business: Get It Done Right!* Irvine, CA: Entrepreneur Press.

Kett, Joseph F. 1994. *Pursuit of Knowledge under Difficulties.* Stanford, CA: Stanford University Press.

Kickham-Samy, Mary. 2010. "Balance of Power and Negotiation of Meaning in Virtual Reference Learning Environments." In *Reference Renaissance: Current and Future Trends,* edited by Marie Radford and R. David Lankes. New York: Neal-Schuman Publishers.

King, David. 2009. *Building the Digital Branch: Guidelines for Transforming Your Library Website.* Chicago: American Library Association.

Kirkpatrick, Donald L. 1998. *Evaluating Training Programs the Four Levels.* San Francisco: Berrett-Koehler.

Klingberg, Susan. 2005. "Information Competencies Checklist: A Resource for Intersegmental Collaboration." *Faculty Publications* (January 1). http://scholarworks.sjsu.edu/lib_pub/2.

Klusek, Louise, and Jerry Bornstein. 2006. "Information Literacy Skills for Business Careers." *Journal of Business & Finance Librarianship* 11, no. 4: 3–21. doi:10.1300/J109v11n04_02.

Kolb, David A. 1984. *Experiential Learning: Experience as the Source of Learning and Development.* Englewood Cliffs, NJ: Prentice-Hall.

Kolter, Philip. 2001. "Atmospherics as a Marketing Tool." *Journal of Retailing* 49, no: 48–65.

Kotter, John P. 1995. "Leading Change: Why Transformation Efforts Fail." *Harvard Business Review* 73, no. 2: 59–67.

Kuhlthau, Carol C. 2004. *Seeking Meaning: A Process Approach to Library and Information Services.* Westport, CT: Libraries Unlimited.

Kuhlthau, Carol C., Jannica Heinström, and Ross J. Todd. 2008. "The 'Information Search Process' Revisited: Is the Model Still Useful?" *Information Research* 13, no. 4: http://informationr.net/ir/13-4/paper355.html.

Kuhlthau, Carol Collier, Leslie K. Maniotes, and Ann K. Caspari. 2012. *Guided Inquiry Design: A Framework for Inquiry in Your School.* Santa Barbara, CA: Libraries Unlimited.

Kuhlthau, Carol Collier, Ann K. Caspari, and Leslie K. Maniotes. 2007. *Guided Inquiry: Learning in the 21st Century.* Westport, CT: Libraries Unlimited.

Kvenild, Cassandra, and Kaijsa Calkins. 2011. *Embedded Librarians: Moving beyond One-Shot Instruction.* Chicago: Association of College and Research Libraries.

Lankes, R. David. 2011. *The Atlas of New Librarianship*. Cambridge, MA, MIT Press: Association of College & Research Libraries.

Lankes, R. David, Scott Nicholson, Marie L. Radford, Joanne Silverstein, Lynn Westbrook, and Philip Nast. 2007. *Virtual Reference Service: From Competencies to Assessment*. Chicago: Neal-Schuman Publishers.

Larson, Jeanette. *CREW: A Weeding Manual for Modern Libraries*. Austin: Texas State Library and Archives Commission. https://www.tsl.state.tx.us/sites/default/files/public/tslac/ld/ld/pubs/crew/crewmethod12.pdf. "Learning Styles Online.com." 2012. *Overview of Learning Styles*. http://www.learning-styles-online.com/.

Leeder, Kim. 2012. "Stop the Snobbery! Why You're Wrong About Community Colleges and Don't Even Know It." Accessed November 19. http://www.inthelibrarywiththeleadpipe.org/2012/stop-the-snobbery/.

"Learning Styles Online.com—Including a Free Inventory." http://www.learning-styles-online.com/.

Liu, Mengxiong. 1995. "Ethnicity and Information Seeking." *The Reference Librarian* 23, no. 49–50: 123–34.

"LOEX Home." http://www.emich.edu/public/loex/.

Lynch, Beverly P., and Kimberley Robles Smith. 2001. "The Changing Nature of Work in Academic Libraries." *College & Research Libraries* 62, no. 5 (September 1): 407–20.

Malvasi, Martina, Catherine Rudowsky, and Jesus M. Valencia. 2009. *Library Rx: Measuring and Treating Library Anxiety: A Research Study*. Chicago: Association of College and Research Libraries.

Massis, Bruce E. 2011. "QR Codes in the Library." *New Library World* 112, no. 9–10: 466–69.

McGowan, Beth. 2011. "Weed, Yes! Discard, No! There May Be a Collection in That Trash!" *Community & Junior College Libraries* 17, no. 2: 87–90. doi:10.1080/02763915.2011.605654.

Meister, Jeanne C., and Karie Willyerd. 2010. "Mentoring Millennials." *Harvard Business Review* 88, no. 5 (May): 68–72.

Merrill, M. David. 2002. "First Principles of Instruction." *ETR&D Educational Technology Research and Development* 50, no. 3: 43–59.

Miller, Shawn. "Take a Minute to Collect Your Thoughts with Evernote." *The Chronicle of Higher Education. ProfHacker*. http://chronicle.com/blogs/profhacker/take-a-minute-to-collect-your-thoughts-with-evernote/24020.

Milner, H. Richard. 2010. "What Does Teacher Education Have to Do with Teaching? Implications for Diversity Studies." *Journal of Teacher Education* 61, no. 1–2: 118–31. doi:10.1177/0022487109347670.

Millson-Martula, Christopher, and John S. Spencer. 2010. *Library transformations: from information commons to learning commons*. Philadelphia: Routledge, Taylor & Francis Group.

Mon, Lorri, and Joseph W. Janes. 2007. "The Thank You Study." *Reference & User Services Quarterly* 46, no. 4 (June 1): 53–59.

Morrison, Gary R., Steven M. Ross, and Jerrold E. Kemp. 2004. *Designing Effective Instruction*. Hoboken, NJ: John Wiley & Sons.

Mullin, Christopher M.2010. "Rebalancing the Mission: The Community College Completion Challenge". American Association of Community Colleges. http://www.aacc.nche.edu/Publications/Briefs/Pages/rb06152010.aspx.

Nahl, Diane, and Dania Bilal. 2007. *Information and Emotion: The Emergent Affective Paradigm in Information Behavior Research and Theory*. Medford, NJ: Information Today, 2007.

National Center for Education Statistics. "Library Statistics Program." http://nces.ed.gov/surveys/libraries/.

National Center for Education Statistics. "National Assessment of Adult Literacy (NAAL)."
    http://nces.ed.gov/naal/literacytypes.asp.

National Endowment for the Arts. 2007. "To Read or Not to Read: A Question of National
    Consequence. Executive Summary." Research Report #47. Washington, D.C.: National
    Endowment for the Arts. http://www.nea.gov/research/ToRead_ExecSum.pdf.

Neal, James G. 2011. "Stop the Madness: The Insanity of ROI and the Need for New Quali-
    tative Measures of Academic Library Success." In *ACRL 2011*. Philadelphia: Associa-
    tion of College and Research Libraries. http://www.ala.org/acrl/sites/ala.org.acrl/
    files/content/conferences/confsandpreconfs/national/2011/papers/stop_the_madness
    .pdf.

"North Carolina College and University Yearbooks. DigitalNC." http://digitalnc.org/
    exhibits/college-yearbooks.

O'Connor, Lisa. 2009. "Information Literacy as Professional Legitimation : A Critical Analy-
    sis." *Journal of Education for Library and Information Science* 50, no. 2: 79–89.
    http://cat.inist.fr/?aModele=afficheN&cpsidt=21258175.

OCLC. "WorldCat Collection Analysis." http://www.oclc.org/collectionanalysis/.
    Onwuegbuzie, Anthony J., Qun G. Jiao, and Sharon L. Bostick. 2004. *Library Anxi-
    ety: Theory, Research, and Applications*. Lanham, MD: Scarecrow Press.

Oud, Joanne. 2008. "Adjusting to the Workplace: Transitions Faced by New Academic
    Librarians." *College & Research Libraries* 69: 252–66.

Overall, Patricia Montiel. 2009. "Cultural Competence: A Conceptual Framework for
    Library and Information Science Professionals." *The Library Quarterly* 79, no. 2:
    175–204.

Pampaloni, Andrea, Bird, Nora J. Forthcoming. "Building Relationships through a Digital
    Branch Library: Finding the Community in Community College Library Web Sites.
    Community College Journal of Research and Practice.

Patterson, David. 2009. "Information Literacy and Community College Students: Using
    New Approaches to Literacy Theory to Produce Equity." *Library Quarterly* 79,
    no. 3: 343–61.

Perrault, Anna H., J. Richard Madaus, and Ann Armbrister. 1999. "The Effects of High
    Median Age on Currency of Resources in Community College Library Collections."
    College & Research Libraries 60, no. 4: 316–39.

Peterson, Lisa C. 1997. "Time Management for Library Professionals." *Katherine Sharp
    Review* 5 (Winter).

Pew Research Center. 2009. "College Enrollment Hits All-Time High, Fueled by Commu-
    nity College Surge." *Pew Social & Demographic Trends*. October 29. http://www
    .pewsocialtrends.org/2009/10/29/college-enrollment-hits-all-time-high-fueled
    -by-community-college-surge/.

Primary Research Group. 2012. *Redesigning the College Library Building*. New York: Primary
    Research Group.

Project Management Institute. 2004. *A Guide to the Project Management Body of Knowledge
    (PMBOK Guide)*. Newtown Square, PA.: Project Management Institute.

Provasnik, Stephen and Planty, Michael. 2008. *Community Colleges: Special Supplement to
    The Condition of Education. Statistical Analysis Report*. Washington, DC: National
    Center for Education. http://nces.ed.gov/pubs2008/2008033.pdf.

Raby, Rosalind Latiner, and Edward James Valeau. 2009. *Community College Models:
    Globalization and Higher Education Reform*. Dordrecht, London: Springer.

Radford, Marie I. 1996. "Communication Theory Applied to the Reference Encounter: An
    Analysis of Critical Incidents." *Library Quarterly* 66, no. 2: 123–37.

Radford, Marie L. 2006. "Encountering Virtual Users: A Qualitative Investigation of Inter-
    personal Communication in Chat Reference." *Journal of the American Society for
    Information Science and Technology* 57, no. 8: 1046–59.

Radford, Marie, and R. David Lankes. 2010. *Reference Renaissance: Current and Future Trends*. New York: Neal-Schuman Publishers.

Ranganathan, S. R. 1957. *The Five Laws of Library Science*. London: Blunt and Sons.

Reference and User Services Association. 2008 "Definitions of Reference." http://www.ala.org/rusa/resources/guidelines/definitionsreference.

Reference and User Services Association. 2004. "Guidelines for Behavioral Performance of Reference and Information Service Providers." http://www.ala.org/rusa/resources/guidelines/guidelinesbehavioral.

Reference and User Services Association "Guidelines for Medical, Legal, and Business Responses," 2001. http://www.ala.org/rusa/resources/guidelines/guidelinesmedical.

Roselle, Ann. 2009. "Preparing the Underprepared: Current Academic Library Practices in Developmental Education." *College & Research Libraries* 70, no. 2: 142–56.

Ross, Catherine Sheldrick, Kirsti Nilsen, and Marie L Radford. 2009. *Conducting the Reference Interview: A How-to-Do-It Manual for Librarians*. New York: Neal-Schuman Publishers.

Ryan, Jenna, Alice L. Daugherty, and Emily C. Mauldin. 2006. "Exploring the LSU Libraries Virtual Reference Transcript: An Analysis." *Electronic Journal of Academic and Special Librarianship* 7, no. 3. http://southernlibrarianship.icaap.org/content/v07n03/ryan_j01.htm.

Schein, Edgar H. 1990. "Organizational Culture." *American Psychologist American Psychologist* 45, no. 2: 109–19.

Schein, Edgar H. 1992. *Organizational Culture and Leadership*. San Francisco: Jossey-Bass.

Schön, Donald. 1989. *Educating the Reflective Practitioner*. San Francisco: Jossey-Bass.

Secker, Jane, and Emma Coonan. *A New Curriculum for Information Literacy: Transitional, Transferable, Transformational*. Cambridge: Cambridge University Library Arcadia Project, 2011. http://ccfil.pbworks.com/f/ANCIL_final.pdf.

Shachaf, Pnina, and Sarah Horowitz. 2006. "Are Virtual Reference Services Color Blind?" *Library & Information Science Research* 28, no. 4 (Winter): 501–20.

Snavely, Loanne. 2004. "Making Problem-Based Learning Work: Institutional Changes." *portal: Libraries and the Academy* 4, no. 4: 521–31.

Society for Human Resource Management (U.S.). 2009. *The SHRM learning system*. Alexandria, VA: Society for Human Resource Management.

Southern Association of Colleges and Schools. Commission on Colleges. 2012. *The Principles of Accreditation: Foundations for Quality Enhancement*. Decatur, GA: Southern Association of Colleges and Schools. http://www.sacscoc.org/pdf/2012PrinciplesOfAcreditation.pdf.

Sterrett, Emily A. 2000. *The Manager's Pocket Guide to Emotional Intelligence from Management to Leadership*. Amherst, MA.: HRD Press.

Stewart, Christopher. 2010. *The academic library building in the digital age: a study of construction, planning, and design of new library space*. Chicago: Association of College and Research Libraries.

Swanson, Troy A. 2004a. "Applying a Critical Pedagogical Perspective to Information Literacy Standards." *Community & Junior College Libraries* 12, no. 4 (2004): 65–77.

Swanson, Troy A. 2004b. "A Radical Step: Implementing A Critical Information Literacy Model." *Portal: Libraries and the Academy* 4, no. 2 (2004): 259–73.

Swords, David A. 2011. *Patron-Driven Acquisitions: History and Best Practices*. Berlin, Boston: De Gruyter Saur.

Taylor, Robert S. 1968. "Question-Negotiation and Information Seeking in Libraries." *College & Research Libraries* 29: 178–94.

Thach, Elizabeth C., and Karen L. Murphy. 1995. "Competencies for Distance Education Professionals." *Educational Technology Research and Development* 43, no. 1: 57–79.

Thomas, Sue, Chris Joseph, Jess Laccetti, Simon Mills, Simon Perril, and Kate Pullinger. 2007. "Transliteracy: Crossing Divides." *First Monday* 12, no. 12. http://www.first monday.org/htbin/cgiwrap/bin/ojs/index.php/fm/article/view/2060/1908.

"Transliteracies: Research Project." 2012. Accessed August 13. http://transliteracies .english.ucsb.edu/category/research-project.

Turley, L., D. Fugate, and R. Milliman. 1990. "Atmospheric Influences on Service Marketing." *Journal of Midwest Marketing* 5 (Spring): 278–86.

21cif.com. "21st Century Information Fluency." http://21cif.com/.

Tyckoson, David. 2003. "On the Desirableness of Personal Relations between Librarians and Readers: The Past and Future of Reference Service." *Reference Services Review* 31, no. 1: 12–16.

Underhill, Paco. 1999. *Why We Buy: The Science of Shopping*. New York: Simon & Schuster.

UNESCO. "Media and Information Literacy." http://portal.unesco.org/ci/en/ev .php-url_id=15886&url_do=do_topic&url_section=201.html.

University Libraries. University of Illinois at Urbana-Champaign. "Digital Literacy Definition and Resources." http://www.library.illinois.edu/diglit/definition.html/.

University Library, University of Illinois at Urbana-Champaign. "Digital Literacy Definition and University of Central Florida. "Information Fluency." *Information Fluency*. http://if.ucf.edu/.

University of North Carolina at Greensboro University Libraries. *Information Literacy Game*. http://library.uncg.edu/game/.

University of North Carolina at Greensboro University Libraries. *Toolkit*. http://uncg .libguides.com/toolkit.

Visser, Michelle. 2003. "Identifying and Caring for Rare Books in the Community or Junior College with No Special Collections Department." *Community & Junior College Libraries* 11, no. 3: 29–34. doi:10.1300/J107v11n03_05.

Walter, Scott. 2008. "Librarians as Teachers: A Qualitative Inquiry into Professional Identity." *College & Research Libraries* 69, no. 1: 51–71.

Wang, Yongming, and Trevor A. Dawes. 2012. "The Next Generation Integrated Library System: A Promise Fulfilled?" *Information Technology and Libraries* 31, no. 3: 76–84. doi:10.6017/ital.v31i3.1914.

Warnken, Paula. 2004. "New Technologies and Constant Change: Managing the Process." *The Journal of Academic Librarianship* 30, no. 4 (July): 322–27. doi:10.1016/ j.acalib.2004.05.001.

Warren, Leslie A. 2006. "Information Literacy in Community Colleges: Focused on Learning." *Reference & User Services Quarterly* 45, no. 4: 297–303.

Watstein, Sarah Barbara, and Steven J. Bell. 2008. "Is There a Future for the Reference Desk? A Point-Counterpoint Discussion." *The Reference Librarian* 49, no. 1: 1–20.

Webber, Desiree, and Andrew Peters. 2010. *Integrated Library Systems Planning, Selecting, and Implementing*. Santa Barbara, CA: Libraries Unlimited. http://site.ebrary.com/ id/10408565.

Whitmire, Ethelene. 1999. "Racial Differences in the Academic Library Experiences of Undergraduates." *The Journal of Academic Librarianship* 25, no. 1: 33–37.

Williams, Shirley. 2012. "40 Social Media Curation Sites and Tools." *Social Media Pearls* . http://socialmediapearls.com/40-social-media-curation-sites-and-tools/.

Willis, Christine A. 2012. "Library Services for Persons with Disabilities: Twentieth Anniversary Update." *Medical Reference Services Quarterly* 31, no. 1: 92–104. doi:10.1080/ 02763869.2012.641855.

Zaleznik, Abraham. 2004. "Managers and Leaders: Are They Different?" *Harvard Business Review* 82, no. 1: 74–81.

Zurkowski, Paul G. (November 1974). "The Information Service Environment Relationships and Priorities. Related Paper No. 5." National Commission on Libraries and Information Science. http://eric.ed.gov/PDFS/ED100391.pdf.

INDEX

Accreditation, 33–37; Collection requirements, 95; Southern Association of Schools and Colleges, 34–36, 44, 61; Use of assessment, 128
Acquisitions, 92
Advocacy, 19, 36, 49, 88, 126
Age, 106
American Association of Community Colleges (AACC), 36–37, 101–2, 106
American Library Association, *Code of Ethics*, 20
Archives, 96
Assessment, 125–31; Collection, 93–94, 116; elements of, 125–31; facilities, 79–80; information literacy, 49; personnel, 138; reference, 23, 29; space, 128; teaching strategies, 59–60. *See also* Standards
Association of College and Research Libraries, 34; Collection standards, 88; Proficiencies for instruction librarians and coordinators, 54

Bibliographic utility. *See* Integrated library system
Budget, 84–85

Career development, 10–12
Cloud, 113; computing, 114–15, 122; cloud-based files, 117
Collection management, 87, 89, 90
Community Outreach, 11, 12, 84

Competencies, job, 10
Construction, 83
Content management systems, 118–21

Degree, requirements for librarian positions, 14, 19
Deselection, 87, 89, 95
Digital library, 98
Digitization, 98, 120
Digitization of unique materials, 98
Distance education, 60
Diversity, 101–11
Donated materials, 89

E-Learning, 115
Embedded librarian, 30–31
Emotional intelligence, 12, 70–75, 109
Evaluation, 59, 61–62

Facilities, 103–4, 126
Faculty, 125, 129, 137
Funding, 37, 84

Gifts. *See* Donated materials
Grant funding, 84
Grants, 97

Hispanic, 143
Human resources, 69; Management, 77; Society of Human Resource Management, 10, 18

ILS. *See* Integrated library system
Information commons, 26
Information literacy, 25, 31, 39–51
Information technology (IT), 8, 123
Institutional repository, 87, 97
Integrated library system (ILS),
  94, 114, 119
Intellectual skills, 134
Interlibrary loan, 8, 14, 85, 90, 95, 119

Job descriptions, 10, 14, 20

Leadership, 11–12, 73, 74–75, 110, 113
Learning management systems, 116
Learning Resource Centers (LRCs), 30, 87
Library collections, 35, 87, 88
LibQUAL+, 129–30
Lifelong learning, 144, 147

Management, 16; meeting, 70; project,
  68–70; skills, 134–36; time, 63–68
Mission, institutional, 35, 88

Open access movement, 91
Open source for integrated library
  systems, 116
Organizational culture, 17–20
Organizational structure, 8–10

Paraprofessionals, 12, 122
Planning, 11, 68–69, 135; event, 9, 12;
  disaster, 85; strategic, 19, 133, 138;
  process, 74
Position classification. *See* Job description
Preservation, 89, 94
Professional Development, 15–17
Project management, 68–70

Quality Enhancement Plans (QEP), 44

Rare books. *See* Special Collections
Reference Desk, 22, 31

Security, 85–86
Special collections, 98
Standards, 33–37
Strategic planning. *See* Planning
Student learning outcomes, 61, 125

Technology: social networks, 43; staffing,
  122; webinars, 116
Tutorials, 115, 116

Virtual: reference, 29; service, 22; spaces, 29

Websites, 53, 110, 117–18
Work study, 122

ABOUT THE AUTHORS

MICHAEL A. CRUMPTON, MLS, SPHR, is the assistant dean for Administrative Services at the University of North Carolina at Greensboro. He is the former director of Library Services for Wake Tech Community College and holds a certificate as a senior human resources professional as well as a graduate certificate in Community College Teaching. His published works include "Workplace Information Literacy: A Neglected Priority of Community College Libraries" in the *Journal of Business & Finance Librarianship*; "Reconceiving Entrepreneurship for Libraries: Collaboration and the Anatomy of a Conference" in *Collaborative Librarianship*; he writes a quarterly column for *The Bottom Line: Managing Library Finances*, and he has published several other chapters and articles.

NORA J. BIRD, MLS, PhD, is an assistant professor in the Department of Library and Information Science at University of North Carolina at Greensboro. She worked as a reference librarian in community and small college libraries in Massachusetts and Connecticut. Her teaching and research interests include collections management and community college libraries, and her published works include "Workplace Information Literacy: A Neglected Priority of Community College Libraries" in the *Journal of Business & Finance Librarianship*; "Source Evaluation and Information Literacy: Findings from a Study on Science Websites" in *Communications in Information Literacy*; "Informationists in a Small University Library" in *Reference & User Services Quarterly*, as well as other articles and proceedings.